Other Books by Charlene Ann Baumbich

Don't Miss Your Kids! (they'll be gone before you know it)
How to Eat Humble Pie & Not Get Indigestion
*Mama Said There'd Be Days Like This (but she never said just
   how many)*

THE 12 DAZES OF CHRISTMAS

(& One Holy Night)

Charlene Ann Baumbich

IVP

InterVarsity Press
Downers Grove, Illinois

InterVarsity Press® is the book-publishing division of InterVarsity Christian Fellowship®, a student movement active on campus at hundreds of universities, colleges and schools of nursing in the United States of America, and a member movement of the International Fellowship of Evangelical Students. For information about local and regional activities, write Public Relations Dept., InterVarsity Christian Fellowship, 6400 Schroeder Rd., P.O. Box 7895, Madison, WI 53707-7895.

Cover and inside illustrations: Tim Nyberg

ISBN 0-8308-1961-4

Printed in the United States of America ♾

Library of Congress Cataloging-in-Publication Data

Baumbich, Charlene Ann, 1945-

   The 12 dazes of Christmas—and one holy night / Charlene Ann Baumbich.

     p.   cm.

   ISBN 0-8308-1961-4 (pbk.: alk. paper)

   1. Christmas.   2. Jesus Christ—Nativity—Devotional literature.
   3. Family—Religious life.   4. Christian life.   5. Baumbich,
   Charlene Ann, 1945-   I. Title.
   BV45.B34 1996
   263'.91—dc20

96-16489
CIP

| 20 | 19 | 18 | 17 | 16 | 15 | 14 | 13 | 12 | 11 | 10 | 9 | 8 | 7 | 6 | 5 | 4 | 3 | 2 | 1 |
| 22 | 21 | 20 | 19 | 18 | 17 | 16 | 15 | 14 | 13 | 12 | 01 | 00 | 99 | 98 | 97 | 96 | | | |

Dedicated to
the real Santa Claus in my life
also known as George John Baumbich

Prologue
When Wonder Turns to Wilt

I am fifty years old. I love Christmas. Santa Claus still comes to my house. Last year I never did get my cards mailed. Images of Christmas Perfection dance in my head like sugarplums (and, yes, I own many slices of them). However, realities of Christmas Crazies zap me like a frog snagging a fly with its tongue—and are about that romantic.

Maybe you know the feeling.

But like me, you have a sincere desire: This will be the year things are different. (Or maybe next year, if you're buying this book during post-Christmas sales.) This will be the year you pull your act together and do Christmas *right*. Right.

Okay, you have promised yourself and your significant others that *for sure,* even though you do not get your act together, this will be the year you find the holy amidst the ho, ho, ho.

Because last year, and the year before (oh, how far back might it go?), the true meaning of Christmas was snuffed out by the whirring, smoking shuffle of the hubbub and blur of the Christmas Season—most of which had nothing to do with the birth of our Lord and Savior. And when you were putting the decorations away (say, near Valentine's Day, if you're really bad), you vowed never to let that happen again. The dark void left in your soul where the shining face of the Christ Child should have beamed is heavy and filled with sorrow. There is a wailing hollowness in which questions swarm.

Where were you, Jesus? Where were you when I was so stressed? Why, during the annual celebration of your birth, weren't you present in my heart?

Why didn't you send an army of angels to help me get everything done so I could spend time thinking about you?

When, Lord, did I stop being filled with awe and wonder at the great miracle given to me and instead start grumbling and grinding my way through the Season?

Where, Dear Lord, did I put the Christmas cards I bought after last year's sale? (Whoops!)

Well, I'm writing this book to let you know, through my personal stories and a few brilliant thoughts, that even though you may never "get your act together," there *is* a way to find the holy in the midst of the chaos.

If you commit to seek his love, and if you pioneer a conscious effort to look, really look, for his face, you will find him. Even in the most unlikely places. And he will restore your energy and renew your faith. He will put a Christmas Gift in your voice that can be freely passed on to others. He will honor every minute you give to him.

He will love you, even when you fail, and that will cause you to love him all the more. He will help you remember what Christmas is *really* about. And that, Dear Reader, is my quest as well.

He will not do your shopping, or buy your tree, or bake your billions of wads of cookies. Neither will I. But he will help you remember why you're doing most of it . . . and perhaps even free you to let some of it go.

"Call to Me, and I will answer you, and I will tell you great and mighty things, which you do not know" (Jeremiah 33:3 NASB). Ya gotta love a promise like that!

Perhaps, when you call, the Christ Child will whisper secret details about his birth. Perhaps he'll show you how to celebrate in the innermost part of your heart and in the outermost part of your life. Perhaps he will birth anew in your spirit.

So pick up your knapsack of hope, and follow me into the land of Christmas stories, where all the episodes (the good, the bad and the dubious) are not picture perfect, but where all the lessons are ripe with his love.

DAZE ONE

The Perfection
(and Other Fables)

The turkey's butt, containing slimy items that should not be baked, is frozen shut. I'm running hot water on it, wondering if we'll all die from some kind of dread turkey germs since I'm thawing it against all "cold water" directions. *So be it; at least there'll never be another miserable morning like this!* It is Christmas Day, and the sounds of Christmas slam and bang throughout my kitchen. I am the one causing the disruption.

I am exhausted and crabby from lack of sleep, and I am being a Martyr. (Yes, with a capital *M*.) You know: "I have to do EVERYTHING! Shopping, wrapping, cards, cooking, baking, invitations, cleaning, laundry . . ." I try not to remind everyone. I fail. They don't want to hear it because they're busy capturing the joy-filled moments of looking for batteries.

I've spent the last two weeks moving from one cashier line to another. They seem to manufacture fewer of everyone's favorite toy just so last-minute Nellies like myself can't simply go to one store and be done. (Nellie is my mother's name, and she could have coined the phrase; it's in my genes!) No, we have to go to thousands of shops before declaring defeat or paying through the nose—which, if you're worn down enough, you're happy to do, just to know there won't be screams of anguish on Christmas day, or worse yet, relentless pouting. And guilt. Let's not forget g-u-i-l-t.

So I have found favorite toys. I've also bought gifts of clothing. But it's a given: most clothes received at Christmas automatically don't fit, especially the cute little things everyone bought for their much-bigger-than-they-thought wife and mother.

At least the Christmas Preparing Phase is, for the most part, over now. But I'm already dreading exchanges and trying to find a place for all the new stuff.

However, I can't worry about that now. I'm too busy invading the cavity of this turkey with the handle end of a wooden spoon, trying to pry it open.

What ever happened to my visions of Christmas Perfecto?

*   *   *

The year is 1954. I am nine years old and it is Christmas Day. The little two-story house on Roselle Road is oozing with the fragrance of roasting turkey laced with eau de balsam fir tree. One scent is stronger than the other, depending on where you stand: in the kitchen, watching Mom happily pile yet more goo-laden pans and cooking utensils on the counter because the sink is already mounded, or in the living room, where little clouds of smoke puff their way out of my brother's new Lionel circling the feet of the getting-pretty-dry-but-oh-how-it-releases-the-fragrance Christmas tree.

Like the turkey and balsam mix, all of the Christmas sights, sounds and activities are stimulating combinations. Knit with the promising clatter and rattle of the tap-dancing kitchen is the joy-filled humming of my mother. The presents have been opened, and Mom overflows with happiness as she glimpses the fire in the sizable new diamond engagement ring Dad just surprised her with. It is a replacement for the tiny ring that announced new promise decades ago when times were rough. The frail band on that ring is worn through. This new token of Dad's love outshines that small but faithful chip of yesteryear. Seems fitting for a love that has so flourished.

The Lionel clouds illuminate with Christmas colors as they skim through bottom branches of the tree and pass over size-seven bulbs. The strong voice of father entwines with the small voice of son in manly murmurings near the engine switch box.

My new blue taffeta dance outfit rustles as I twirl, twirl—I am not merely beautiful in this princess-ly costume that billows around me; as I drape and pose myself across the back of an overstuffed chair, I *am* beauty itself.

Sparkling tufts of wrapping paper and loops of ribbon lap at our ankles like red and green waves in a sea of holiday. We push and kick them around, mindless of the mess, in fact quite happy nesting in the remnants of bounty.

All nerve endings hone, capture and pulse with every vital beat of the magic and mystery of Christmas energies. I have nothing to do but greedily gulp down the moments and wallow in the joy.

*   *   *

The year is 1951 and I am six. It is the day after Christmas. We have made our annual Christmas pilgrimage to Grandma and Grandpa's farm in southern Illinois. We are all trying to get ourselves organized in the overcrowded living room for a group photo: Great-granddad Landers, with the thick, twirly mustache; Grandma Landers, who bristles with activity, and Grandpa, whose eyes twinkle as he tells yet another story; Aunt Del and Uncle Pookie and J. R., their son, the same age as myself and tired of standing still and saying cheese; Mom, Dad (who is taking the picture), my baby brother, Jimmy, and me.

Even if Santa hadn't come again to this place—which he did—I would have had a jolly good time, for life at the farm is

17

pure gold. Especially when you are the visitor and have none of the farm chores to do.

Cousin J. R. and I bath cross-legged in galvanized tubs out on the enclosed porch. Grandma prepares this royal opportunity by first pouring boiling water from the kettle into our awaiting tubs, then tempering it with rain water scooped out of the barrel. Only when it is just right may we ooze in.

We squirt a bar of soap back and forth through the air from tub to tub and giggle all the while, especially when it hits the floor and goes skittering into a nook or cranny. Then we have to carefully birth ourselves out of the warm cocoon and freeze to death while scurrying, buck naked, to capture it.

Mom braids my thin, wet hair afterward, and J. R. and I are off and running again until it is time for bed.

Nothing in this world is as soft as a feather bed when you're six. We scurry up the enclosed staircase, anticipating the adventure that awaits us, for at the top of the stairs is older second cousin Harry, who always seems to have the bed warmed, and sharing is a must. Nothing causes more raucous tumbling or more pillow fights than crawling under the covers and pulling the hair on his "Harry the Hairy" legs.

Fun is invented just for us. There is nothing to do but embrace it with all our might.

* * *

No matter how far back in my growing-up years I recall, Christmas was enchanted. I am thankful for not only the times, but the people, the places, the joy. Most of those loved ones are gone now, including my mother, but the endearing memories set a tone for every anticipated Christmas season that approaches.

And that is the beginning of my personal slippery slide into Christmas Disappointment. For you see, in all those childhood memories, I had nothing—NOTHING—to do to prepare for it. Christmas just happened. Wow, has *that* ever changed.

* * *

For many people, there never were those happy memories. Christmas was always a disappointment, even a heartache. Alcohol, poverty, mean people. Forgotten requests, loud relatives, arguments. And so they clung to the hope that when they grew up, Christmas would one day be the stuff of Hallmark Hall of Fame presentations. Everything, if it wasn't peachy now, eventually would be. People would change. Money would come. Families would be united in love and understanding. They put that in their memory banks and said, "*That's* how Christmas will one day be for me."

And that is the beginning of the slippery slope for them, which isn't much different than my own dreams of perfection. We think we know what Christmas *should* be. Sadly, we forget, at least for the most part, what Christmas *is*.

In even my best of childhood memories, did you notice a key factor was missing? Where are my memories of pondering the fact that it was the birth of the Christ Child we were celebrating? Where is the picture of the family sharing stories about Jesus and what he meant in our own family?

Sure, most of us in our culture attend church plays (maybe we're even in them) and services. We sing carols and for the moment *feel* Christmas. But is the celebration of the birth of Jesus the hook we hang our hearts on? The Dream Vision we long and pray for? The goal? And if it was, wouldn't *that* rearrange our expectations? For what could be missing if Jesus was all we desired?

DAZE TWO

The List
(All I Want for
Christmas)

L ists. They are endless during the holidays. Shopping lists. Invitation lists. Christmas card lists.

And there are the ongoing lists—ordinary things to do aside from Christmas stuff, like preparing dinner (or talking to the speaker at the drive-through window) and dropping off the dry cleaning and paying the insurance bill. And often, when someone else crosses something off their list, it was something they needed to tell you to do, so it gets added to your already mongo-sized liturgy.

Then Christmas Day finally arrives, and with great relief you tear up the last of your lists. Until you begin the "Things to Return and/or Exchange" list. And the new shopping list that springs from reading the after-Christmas sale flyers. Items like Christmas bulb replacements, since your tree is terribly dim and only the bottom halves of your outdoor bushes are flashing. And hey, why not stock up on wrapping paper for next year? And cards, although you need to make a written note on a list someplace as to where you put them.

These lists are no sooner put to bed than—BHAM!—it's time to begin next year's shopping list. This early-bird list is prompted by the constant, in-your-face display of Christmas catalog pages (catalogs mailed before the Fourth of July) by the children in or near your life. Closing your eyes doesn't help, because their eardrum-piercing screams still invade the guilt-inducing lobe of your brain. Screams of "I WANT that! I GOTTA have this!" incited by television commercials that play directly to the Greed Zone in their toddler-to-adolescent brains.

The children's wish list can be summarized like this:

Everything on pages 3 to 87.

Everything I see advertised during waking hours.

No holiday lists are simple. They are always cursed by dilemmas. I listened last year as a friend tried to discern when, exactly, you cut a relative off a Christmas gift list. Tricky business, this relative stuff, especially as kids grow up.

The progression goes something like this: Your siblings or friends get married and begin cranking out kids. You of course buy the little darlings gifts. After all, you like being Uncle or Aunt Somebody, and they think you're pretty cool. They are small and cute and thankful for any wild or trendy thing you come up with.

Then they get a little older, and it gets trickier, not only to pick something out, but to please them. After several "tilt" years, you resort to cash, because you know it's what they really want, and you're trying to simplify your life.

Then they begin entering that gray area of adulthood, maybe

even take off for college. Something inside you says, "Okay, they're grown now. I never even see them anymore. It's time to take them off my list." But how do you cut one off without snuffing their siblings? Is it fair to oust just one because, due to circumstances beyond their control, they have passed some arbitrary age line that cuts them off your list? And how do you approach this subject with their family?

This is even more complicated if you have fewer, or worse yet, no children of your own to benefit from this "exchange." Is it fair that year after year you're shelling out tons o'bucks while getting nothing in return? This is the stuff drawing names is made of.

And how about those Christmas card lists? How many of you keep the tit-for-tat kind? Just how many years do you keep sending someone a card who never sends you one? And why is it that the year you finally cut somebody out, that's the year they jump back in the cycle? Did you guilt them into it? Were you trying to hang on to a friendship that had passed its time? And do you really want to put a check by their name when, after all these years, they didn't even put a note in the card?

Each year you check that card list, and even though, to save on ever-increasing postage, you've finally excised the people you see every day (and you tell them this every day so they'll understand your logical thinking and so you won't traumatize their egos—but they keep sending you cards anyway, adding to your guilt), somehow the list keeps getting longer. (It's one of the laws of the universe: *All lists keep getting longer.*)

Then there is your own personal Christmas Wish List, which you wish someone, anyone, would ask you for, although in its own way it's starting to smack of "everything from pages 3 to 87."

Oh, maybe your husband says, "What do you want for Christmas?" But you don't want to *tell* him; you want him to *know*. You want him to have paid attention to you back in March when you were lusting over a wonderful silver bracelet that had hearts on it and you said, "Maybe Santa will get me that."

You hoped he was listening in August when you said, "You know what I'd really lo-o-o-ove? A day at a beauty spa. An entire day of pampering, just for me. That would be a great Christmas

25

gift, honey. Easy shopping for you too. You could just phone this number and order a gift certificate." Maybe you even left the half-page ad lying in his favorite chair, and when it finally disappeared, you were just sure he'd taken it to his secret hiding place and added it to his list. Right.

I'll admit to actually circling items in sale flyers, to putting monster arrows in the margins. I've left my list on the counter, on the kitchen table, on top of his dresser. I've pointed to things in windows the beginning of the third week in December and said, "That's ALL I really want for Christmas."

Still, I don't really want him to ask me what I want, nor do I want to tell him. I just want him to *know*.

One of the lists that becomes most important to me is "Gifts Already Bought." The last several years I've actually begun buying presents right after Christmas, and I continue throughout the spring, summer and fall. Not lots. Not with intention, but cool stuff I stumble across that happens to be on sale, especially if it's something fun.

I try to keep a master list of all the people I have to *(desire to* mixed with *have to;* we'll discuss that later) get something(s) for. Then I write each gift down as I purchase it, and I store the find in this large white plastic bag upstairs. My master list gets lots of action. There are a couple of columns that need to stay pretty equal, especially since our personal family tradition has converted over the years from mass-hysteria opening to taking turns—and it's important that everyone come out even. After several years, this master list eventually gets so worn that I have to make a new one, which is as terrible as finally realizing you need to make a new Christmas card list because you've used up every last empty space changing addresses and putting people back on and taking them off again. And the problem with that, at least for me, is that I never—*never*—throw away my old list. Because I'll probably be retrieving names and addresses off it in the near future.

Oh, the ravages of lists! The beastly addiction to their necessity! The sinister consumption of our time in keeping track of them!

The lie! For Christmas shouldn't be about lists.

How far have we come since the time when a star shone bright in the sky and beamed into our human eye, awakening our spirit and causing us to follow? Never mind any lists. Never mind any material desires. All we need to do is respond to the star's all-consuming glow. It is then we find ourselves face to face with the Christ Child.

Follow. Drop everything and come. Bring only what is in your heart. Look. Listen. See on my face all innocence and righteousness; it is yours for the asking. Know that I am the Lamb of God who takes away the sins of the world. Know that my blood will flow red and my gift to you is evergreen. Know that I was born into the kingdom for you. Be still and know that I Am. Give to me all your burdens, all your desires, all your lists.

Do not lean on your own understanding about the holiday; just look into my eyes and rest in them, knowing they are watching over all that matters, really matters, from this day forward until I come again.

But for now we must remember that he came the first time. Is that on your list?

DAZE THREE

The Traditions
(Santa and More)

"Tra-di-tion!" I can hear Tevye in *Fiddler on the Roof* bellowing that line as the music begins to thump and pulse in the background. Tradition is important to the human spirit. It is the stuff we build the rest of our lives on. It is the way things should be.

"But that's the way things have always been done at our

house!" (Or in our religion, nationality, family.)

"This tradition races through my blood."

I can hear spouses saying this to one another as they come face to face with the horrid reality that their traditions—especially Christmas traditions—are about as polarized as real versus instant mashed potatoes. You either believe in them or you don't. And woe unto the family that cannot compromise or build new ones. (In the case of mashed potatoes, I say real mashed potatoes win. And if you don't agree, then the only compromise is no potatoes. Although, if I am a guest at your home during the holidays and you serve me instants, I will happily eat them, because anything I don't have to prepare is fine with me.)

Webster's *New World Dictionary* has five explanations of the word *tradition*. The most common definition is "the handing down orally of stories, beliefs, customs, etc. from generation to generation."

But I believe this definition gets more to the root of things when it comes to Christmas: "A long-established custom or practice that has the effect of an unwritten law."

Law. Big word. Which leads us to yet a couple of other Webster's tidbits we might find interesting as we prepare, for better or for worse, to hold on to our traditions. You know, the *right* way. Here's one: "L. *tradito,* to deliver: see TREASON." "1. orig., a surrender or betrayal."

Treason. Betrayal. Now these words ring all our bells as we screech about the heresy of the tradition upon which another's family has been reared.

"Don't even *think* about suggesting we carry on with that ridiculous agenda!"

"Why, *why* would you want to keep the kids up for midnight services when you know they'll be cranky all day?"

"What do you mean we *have* to have Christmas dinner at *your* mother's?"

"No one opens their gifts Christmas Eve! Santa doesn't arrive until after midnight!"

"You have noodles and peas? No broccoli?"

"Ham? Turkey is what people have on Christmas!"

"I don't care if it is the only time you all get together. All you do is argue anyway! Why cling to *that?*"

31

"Real trees are a fire hazard."

"Fake trees are an act of treason."

"Christmas lights are not supposed to flash; they are supposed to just quietly glow."

"Your mom's pie crust is terrible. Why don't I give her my mom's recipe?"

"There is no Santa Claus, nor will there ever be in our house."

"Drawing names is so impersonal."

"You spend *how* much money on your family?"

"A vegetarian Christmas dinner? Get a life."

"All that meat and gravy will kill you. Can't you just feel each swallow clogging your arteries on the way down?"

"The tree doesn't go up until Christmas Eve."

"The tree goes up December 1."

"But we always see the *Nutcracker.*"

"Football is the stuff the holidays are made of."

"I hate Christmas."

"Christmas is my *favorite* time of the year."

Christmas traditions are comforting routines that help us remember that some things almost never change. Whether it's a mild winter with no snow or we're buried in the glistening white stuff, a Christmas morning fire melds dried logs and crumpled wrappings, warming our bodies and quieting our hearts with its smoky fragrance and crackling sound.

Then there's Santa, perhaps the biggest tradition of them all. Amidst fashion swings and political upheaval and death and destruction and time changes, just before we finally go to bed on Christmas Eve, I still read *The Night Before Christmas* to my adult boys if they're home for the holidays. I study the familiar illustrations of the Santa-shaped, dog-eared book and relish the rhyming words, which I have memorized but read anyway.

It doesn't matter how tired I am or how old anyone in this family gets, Santa still comes in the middle of the night—for everyone!

Mysteriously, gifts crowd their way under and around the tree, and we are always surprised by some of Santa's selections. One year the old guy got me a power drill. Imagine!

Santa, that dear man whose handwriting would resist analysis because his alphabetical letters appear in so many different slants and shapes within our household (and in so many languages throughout the world).

And speaking of letters, Santa still writes them to the boys of this house. Santa, like a puppet, seems more free to speak tender words from the heart that are often difficult for mortal humans to release. Santa recalls all that was accomplished by the individual during the year (since his job is spying), and speaks of how proud he (she) is. Santa has a swell sense of humor and occasionally reminds the boys of an adventure that ran amuck but has been transformed into yet another great family story, now that we have the perspective of time and healing.

The main Santa in our house writes these letters in the late quiet of Silent Night as she gazes upon the face of the Christ Child traditionally arranged in full nativity regalia on a living-room shelf. Our nativity figures are iridescent white, and they reflect the mood of this greatest of sparkling, life-transforming gifts.

Our family Santa sometimes weeps as she allows the serenity and love of Jesus to wash through her fingers and onto the paper in an expression of love and gratefulness from mother to sons.

34

Now, Santa is not to be confused with Jesus; one is real, the other isn't. One is the reason for the true Christmas celebration; the other is a product of folklore and merchandising. One is the King of kings, and the other is a figment of imagination, albeit a figment whose presence in our personal traditions helps pass on a spirit of giving.

As a child, believing in Santa, whom I could occasionally see, was for me a great emotional warm-up to being able to believe in the living Christ, whom I could not see. By the time I had to come to grips with the fact that there was no real Santa Claus, God—through his Holy Word, the awakening of my spirit and the actions of his followers around me—had proven to me his realness. His Spirit lived in my heart.

This year, however, the two came together in an unimaginable way: Christ used the mortal body of a Santa to speak to me.

* * *

For a long time I've wanted to have my picture taken with Santa as a gift to my boys, who I knew would appreciate Mom's sense of fun and adventure. (Right, boys? And if you don't, remember Santa is watching, and Santa will be miffed to learn you don't have those photos of Mom and Santa prominently displayed in your homes, thereby causing Santa to perhaps reevaluate next year's stocking loot!) But the last few years, when I've happened upon a Santa in a mall, the lines have always been too long and I've been in too big a hurry to follow through on this whim.

This year was different. I found Santa alone but for an elf (the photographer), one baby on his lap and two parents hurling themselves around like goons trying to get their precious one to smile. Inclement weather and hazardous road conditions opened this opportunity. And so I seized the moment and told the elf I'd like to have my picture taken, using the holiday special rate of one five-by-seven and two wallet-size photos for under $10. Big George could take the five-by-seven to his office. (Ditto goes to George about the loot!) The elf asked my name and told me the obvious: I would be next—as soon as the threesome either got a good picture or expired from their aerobic drama. (My words, not the elf's.)

"Santa, this is Charlene. She'd like to have her picture taken with you."

"Well, hello, Charlene. Come talk to Santa." He was kind; his face registered no shock or scorn.

"Santa, my gift to you will be that I won't sit on your lap; I'll sit on the cushion next to you."

No arguments from Santa.

The two of us cuddled up for the photo and the flash blinked, announcing completion of my mission.

"Charlene, what would you like Santa to bring you for Christmas?" Santa asked.

I hadn't thought this far ahead; the photo was all I'd wanted. (Not thinking ahead is something I'm famous for, but then, Santa probably already knew that.)

Without batting an eye or hesitating for a moment, the following—which was total truth—erupted from my lips on this particular Friday.

"Santa, I'm having a hysterectomy next Wednesday, and I'd like swift healing." Although I couldn't believe what I'd uttered, I was not surprised, as this disbelief of my own utterings is routine.

Then Santa's blue eyes looked straight into mine, as though

they were piercing my soul. He said, "I'll pray for you, and so will Mrs. Claus."

I was so moved that I immediately began to cry. "Oh, Santa, you couldn't have told me anything more perfect." Realizing that I was now standing before him bawling, I added, "Perhaps more estrogen would be nice too."

Santa smiled. I thanked him one last time and walked away, but not before saying, "You know, you still come to my house in the middle of the night every year, even though my baby is twenty-five years old."

"I know," he replied.

Well, the photos were swell. But they were secondary to my experience. I told nearly everyone I saw about my meeting with Santa. "It was as though Christ became incarnate in this Santa to assure me that everything would be okay," I heard myself repeating time after time. "I felt so calm." My friend Janet, a sister in Christ whom I'd told, faxed me before surgery to let me know she was praying for me. She prayed that my surgery go as scheduled. She prayed for my recovery, for my relationships to be blessings to me and God, for the doctors to have wisdom. And "I pray," she wrote, "that Mr. and Mrs. Claus have their prayers answered." She too had been affected by my story.

As it turned out, surgery went pretty well. Two hours after surgery, however, my heart rate began to drop—all the way to zero, which, as one doctor said, "we thought was a little too low." I became a flat-liner on the monitors (which means you're well on your way to dead), and nurse Jaci had to administer CPR. I snapped right back, thanks to the grace of God and Jaci's quick actions. I have recuperated just fine.

But I cannot begin to tell you how many times during and since my recovery I've revisited my encounter with Santa. I am in awe of how I felt so blessed and lifted right into the presence of Jesus when Santa talked to me. In fact, God's arms, looking very much like Santa's, can be seen wrapped around me in the photo. Of this I am sure.

* * *

Occasionally a new tradition simply evolves in a family. Many years ago, Santa left me a garment-shaped package under the tree. It was quite hefty. As I shook it, I loudly speculated all kinds of dazzling, expensive things. Paper flew left and right as I ripped the lovely packaging (hand-made bow) off in a flurry.

What to my wondering eyes should appear but four Charleston Chew candy bars! I had recently gone through a spell of craving Charleston Chews, as opposed to my usual chip-and-dip attacks, and Santa had cleverly been paying attention. I screeched and hollered with great glee, then ran right to the refrigerator to freeze them. (I especially love cracking them apart to eat them.) Santa had delighted my heart, and it showed.

The next year, Santa left me a tube-shaped gift. Guess what was inside this camouflaged paper towel roll? Right! Every year since, Santa mischievously goes to great pains to make me think that the package I'm about to open might contain a precious commodity. He has used bricks; he has used giant boxes with little boxes inside. My thoughtful George—er, I mean Santa—and the Charleston Chews tradition.

Inexpensive. Fun. Heart-warming. Fattening! New traditions don't have to be taxing, just meaningful. They can be personal, they can be silly—and they will be repeated year upon year.

* * *

Some old traditions have changed in my family, and one change in particular didn't come easily. I think I can best tell you about it in the form of the prayer I lifted to the Lord. It was the day Santa Charlene talked to Jesus.

Dear Lord,

Bret told me weeks ago, in a very quiet tone, that he couldn't come home for the holidays this year. I cried when I hung up. I'd kept a level tone in my voice as long as I could.

I thought I had worked it all through in my heart. After all, I had him with me for twenty Christmases . . . and all the days between. Then he moved halfway across the country for a new job. Remember how I mourned then? But at least he came home for Christmas.

This last year, I started to get used to his absence. We talk often on the phone. (By the way, thanks so much for sending Alexander with his "reach out and touch someone" invention.) And I did get to visit him in October. I even started believing Christmas wouldn't be so terrible without him . . . until today. Today, after we brought the Christmas boxes down and un-

packed our years of treasures.

Wreaths were hung on doors, ornaments were placed on tree limbs, and lights were strung almost everywhere there was a socket. I was humming "Joy to the World." Then I came to the bottom of the last box. Oh, my sweet Lord, what will I do with his Christmas stocking?

For twenty years it has hung on the mantel. I can remember holding my wide-eyed babe up to it and jabbering on and on about what Santa had left him.

Then came the best of years for stockings, when children stumble down the stairs before dawn and see those first package corners peeking out at them.

One Christmas morning we were awakened by Bret at 3:30 with the news of Santa's arrival. It is truly a blessing how memories can be fonder than their reality. That was the year we made a new rule: If either one of the boys was up before 5:30 a.m. (and guaranteed it would be Bret), he could open the top gift in his stocking, if he didn't wake anyone else until six.

Once Santa was no longer admitted (though never really denied), the stocking became the dwelling place for small treas-

ures: *jewelry, photos, gifts from the heart. It was my favorite place to buy for, and often brought the most Christmas fun. Like the year I got Bret a nose harp. He had a blast entertaining us with that. Tune after spontaneous tune was generated by the air he squirted out of his nose into the receptacle in the nose harp. And it was certainly a gift no one wanted to borrow! Of course I still stashed our family's traditional three quarters, one tangerine and five walnuts in the toe. He expects that, but he always acts surprised, just for me.*

Now, Lord, the stocking lies here in my lap while all these memories march by. I have become paralyzed with—I'm not sure what. I can't bear to see it hanging, knowing there will be no one to unwrap its contents. No laughter. No surprises.

What's that you say, Lord? Sounds like I don't have hope? You know I do. You gave it to me. You have given me everything, including my son. Most importantly, you gave me yours, and that's what I need to remember now. Forgive me, Lord, for my sorry human nature.

You're right. This stocking doesn't represent loneliness. It is filled with twenty years of joy. It contains the fingerprints of a lifetime of sharing and growing with the son you gave me. And it marks the season we celebrate the Greatest Gift of All—the Gift of Your Love. Your Son.

Thank you, Lord, for listening (as you always do, day and night) and setting me straight. The stocking will be hung by the chimney with care, in hope . . . in hope that it will remind me of all I have been given, including this stocking full of memories.

No, I can't be with him, but you are. You, who always know when he's naughty or nice (even when he's out of my sight) and love him endlessly anyway. Just like you do me. And it is you, Lord, who will carry me through this time of pain and adjustment. In fact, you already are.

Amen.

*   *   *

That wasn't the only time Bret has been absent for the holidays. After much angst and further years of the dilemma, I finally relinquished the stocking and sent it to him, once and for all. When he does come home, he can bring it, and by some mystery Santa will know where to find it. And I know the day will come when Brian, who still journeys home from Minnesota, will have his own traditions or plans or family to tend to and George and I will be alone.

But Jesus will be with us as we work to remember and celebrate the Old Traditions and seek to embrace the New. If marriage and children should be a part of our boys' lives, perhaps we'll even go to *their* families' homes, sit in *their* living rooms and eat *their* food. *Their* mess to clean up. Hey, I could easily adapt to that idea!

Yes, Christmas should be a potent reminder that some things never change: God is sovereign, Jesus saves and old Christmas carols never die. The Christ Child was born, lived, died, was buried and raised again from the dead. But first he was a child, and this is what we celebrate.

But it is *only* God who never changes. And it is only Jesus who can help our hearts when circumstances and traditions do.

DAZE FOUR

The Tree
(Prepare for Battle!)

One afternoon when we were all together a few Christmas holidays ago, we lugged out our box of photographs and tried to put them in some kind of order. Now don't get too excited; all this really meant was making several small piles out of one jumbled boxful. I then rubberbanded the smaller piles to keep them from shuffling back into one another and repacked them in separate corners of the box. Although I may be Organizationally Challenged, I do occasionally make attempts to move toward a cure.

Since George and I have lived in the same house our entire twenty-seven married years, it was fun to watch the decorating motif change in the photos from Early Halloween to Southwest Stuff to College-Bills Worn to Mid-Life Redecorated, and then to our current We're-in-the-Middle-of-Updating-the-Redecorating. (We've been saying that for two years now.)

One stack of photos became The Christmas Stack. What fun we had comparing all the sizes and shapes—not only of the Christmas trees, but of ourselves. My, how we've all grown (ready or not), even Wonderdog Butch.

The first couple of years of photos show the tree (of course) in front of the picture window. It's what we imagined when we bought the place. Probably influenced our purchase more than we might think, this stunning setting for a Christmas tree. However, the reality was that no matter how we tried to arrange the furniture to accommodate it, we couldn't see each other around the tree.

After several years of neck craning, we tried the northwest corner near the front door and moved the television to the south wall. Since we'd finally purchased two lounge chairs and placed them on either side of the fireplace on the east wall, we could feel the warmth while looking at the tree. This seemed ideal until we realized that putting the TV on the south wall meant that the only people who could watch it were those passing by our picture window.

So the following year we moved the tree next to the fireplace, the television to the other side of the fireplace and our new L-shaped couch down by the entryway. Putting the tree next to the fireplace worked because that was the year we bought an artificial tree. As of this writing, we still carry on with this configuration.

Our trees have ranged from Charlie Brown scraggly to major lush and giant. Giant enough to envelop most of the living room. First place in our size contest was one more in the shape of a triangle than a tree, but I loved its girth and bountiful ability to present, in uncrowded abandon, our years of treasured ornaments.

My vision of Christmas Tree Perfecto was shaped, in part, by my annual childhood excursions to Marshall Field's department store in Chicago. The Walnut Room restaurant on the seventh floor houses a stunning theme Christmas tree which annually matches the theme of the holiday window decorations. (Several years ago Bret had an all-Elvis tree at his house; maybe I should call Field's with that idea.) Part of our fun was not only viewing the tree—from several different floors—but eating grown-up food at its feet. We even dressed up for the occasion.

Also, the large living room in the farmhouse where I grew up had ample room for king-size trees, and so we had them. Yes, for me, bigger was always better, and I've had my share of those during our married years.

For George, small and less expensive is perfect. Not so much hassle wrestling it around and sawing to make it fit in the stand. No cranes needed to get the star on the top. Fewer lights. We've had our share of those trees as well.

The boys always voiced their criteria: Lots of room for presents underneath! Which, of course, leaned them toward my

49

large-tree way of thinking.

I hope it hasn't gone unnoticed that George and I have different tastes and opposite priorities when it comes to Christmas trees. This has caused no small amount of distress over the years as we head for tree lots. I have always been willing to spend lots on a tree, since we only purchase one a year. I have this wonderful gift (although George certainly doesn't see it that way) of being able to mentally amortize expenditures over long periods of time. If a tree cost $50 (which we have never spent, but if we did), you could simply amortize that over, say, sixty years, since you might live that long and that's how many years you could relish the memory of this special tree. It's less than a dollar a year for the beauty of a moment that you will remember for the rest of your life. See how it works?

George, on the other hand, knows that no tree is worth more than they charge on the cheapest lot. "$9.99—Your Pick." Now we're talking, right, George? So that is where we would begin, and yes, sometimes end up, but not until hours of precious tree-buying trauma were behind us.

But first let me talk about how we prepared for this annual excursion.

"We're not going to buy a tree too big for the living room again, are we?" George is trying to set boundaries as he heads toward the closet for his coat.

"Well, I'm sure not excited about getting one that looks like a houseplant. Remember the time we couldn't get half our ornaments on that splinter of a tree we bought?" I'm trying to counter with reasonable limits as I cram my arms into my coat sleeves.

George says, "The sign at Kmart says any tree for $12.99. They look pretty nice. Let's go there."

"Okay. But I'm not getting a tree I hate just because it's $12.99. Remember the year that cheap tree was so dry that its branches folded up like an umbrella and swallowed the ornaments? Remember how we were afraid to turn the lights on two days after we put it up? Remember how we were nearly cut to ribbons trying to reach through the dried needles to retrieve our treasures?" I'm already standing my ground, and we haven't left the driveway yet.

"They all cut the trees in the middle of summer. Paying more money doesn't mean a fresher tree."

"Well, it seems to me that our more expensive finds have lasted longer."

"Just luck, if that's true. But I don't think it is."

"Let's stop squabbling. This is supposed to be fun." We both honor the truth in that, at least for a moment.

We corral the boys and hit the road. We're on our way to Kmart's tree lot, and George is singing a Christmas-tree-buying song he's inventing. This is very out-of-character behavior for George, and it's actually a pretty funny little ditty. For a while I believe that this year things may be different.

By the time we're almost there, it wouldn't matter if we were arguing anyway, because we could no longer hear each other's rumblings. Why? Because we've all tugged on our earmuffs and scarves: we've waited until the coldest day of the year to bag our prey. Odds are there's also been a freezing rain that morning, so by the time we get to the lots the little trees are frozen shut. No amount of hammering and banging will give us a peek into their fluffed-up possibilities.

But the four of us scatter anyway, each calling out when a potential winner is spotted. We all move toward the sound of a familiar voice. From the end of the aisle, without even coming close, two of us already don't like it. We notice its trunk looks like a visual aid for the letter *S* on a *Sesame Street* show.

Again we disperse and thrash through a few more rows. What looks like the perfect find ends up to have no limbs on one side. Some years this is the good news, if you're cramming it in a corner. On the other hand, what if when it thaws out it's even more sparse than it looks while slammed shut? Better keep looking.

Too fat, too small, too tall. Wrong type (we like short needles, but not too short); wrong concept; just wrong. By consensus we decide it's time to try another lot. This happens more than once. We're freezing to death.

Finally there's one we all like, but you pay by the foot, and although its shape is perfect, we would have to cut nearly three paid-for feet off the bottom to get it to stand upright. This definitely doesn't sit well with George. I've been married to him long enough that I see his point. This worries me.

There comes a time when we all just can't take it any more, because we're worried about frostbite, and a tree—not perfect, but acceptable (at least by three of us, and the other guy is outnumbered), is crammed in the truck or strapped on top the car.

No matter how thorough we've been, we've ended up with trees that zigged and zagged, and trees that had to be tied up because they simply would not balance right, and trees that had to be considerably lopped off at the bottom. We've even had a few from which we just didn't have the heart to excise the lush lower branches, so we lopped off the top and kind of buried our star or angel or whatever in the Y.

If only the decisions were finally over, but no. Now we have the tinsel or garland debate. Or how about those silver and red beads?

And the Slinkies? One year, in a fit of Victorian influence, I bought dozens of gold, shiny, springy things that reflect the lights. They're beautiful, but just try and put them away at the end of the year. They tangle around one another faster than a tackle box full of fishing lures without any dividers. We had to wrap them individually, and I just haven't had the stamina to deal with them again.

The number of ornaments we put on has expanded and shrunk with the size of the tree. It's like rediscovering buried gold each year when I fold back the tissue paper on the extra-special ones. We have ornaments the kids made when they were in school and Scouts. There are dated ornaments given by friends and lots of crafted creations made by the boys and me. There are clip-on, hand-blown glass birds that used to be my mom and dad's when they were first married. Of course there are boxes of trendy new glass ornaments that add color and brightness. And how could we forget the glow-in-the-dark icicles, and the four plastic angels, and my singing hippopotamus, and the dancing pig?

Purchasing an artificial tree years ago was traumatic for me, but it was time to do it, and it has really simplified things. Although our tree looks pretty much the same from year to year now, I do enjoy its sturdiness and the fact that I don't have to worry about it drying out. We can put it up whenever we feel like prowling through our basement and dealing with it, and we can dismantle it without wearing protective clothing.

It usually takes us two or three days to finish the tree. When we finally do, I'm happy for its beauty.

But never once has our family tree outdone what God created in a forest. Not one can match the stunning beauty and fragrance of a stately Ponderosa Pine high atop the Jemez mountains in New Mexico.

Park yourself in front of a decades-old blue spruce, and marvel at its stalwart beauty. Study each needle on one branch; rub them between your fingers, releasing the natural gifts. Inhale. Say a prayer of thanksgiving to a God who freely gave you all this beauty. A prayer of thanksgiving for his Son, who gives it all meaning. A prayer of thanksgiving for this quiet moment in front of the tree that needed nothing from you but noticing.

When we had an ice storm last year, and glistening beams of sparkling light moved and crackled with the rhythm of the wind as it rocked the ice-laden branches along our street, I thought of our Christmas trees that take so much effort and energy. So much squabbling and time. And I almost wondered why we bother. Why not just come, sit in a snowy forest or bicycle down a wooded path, and drink it all in.

    O Christmas tree, O Christmas tree,
    How lovely are thy branches! . . .
    Its boughs are broad, its leaves are green;
    It blooms for us when wild winds blow,
    And earth is white with feath'ry snow;
    A voice tells all its boughs among
    Of shepherd's watch and angel's song;
    Of holy Babe in manger low,
    The story of so long ago.

DAZE FIVE

The Decorating
(Every Nook
and Cranny)

For the last three years I have been paring down the Christmas decorations. I'm happy to report we now only have to lug ten large boxes from the attic, this after a record-breaking thirteen. I am not including in this count the tree box and giant wreath we store in the basement.

I find that at age fifty I am overwhelmed by the amount of Christmas stuff we've accumulated, and I'm doing my best to get it under control. Of course I'm also, at age fifty, occasionally overwhelmed by the lid on a bottle of aspirin, so how seriously should I take myself?

Three of the boxes and part of another are full of tree trimmings. The rest are crammed with everything from Christmas towels to table decorations to the eight-inch, twenty-piece nativity scene plus stable.

We also have a nearly empty roll of Christmas toilet paper tucked away in one of the miscellaneous boxes. Mom gave it to us twenty-two years ago, the year before she died. We used most of it when company came to visit. It was a great conversation piece because the ladies were always all atwitter as to whether they might be dying their bottoms red and green when they used it. I just cannot bear to throw away the core with the few remaining tissues. You now know why we have ten large boxes.

This is how anyone accumulates too much Christmas stuff. Nearly everything has a memory wrapped around it. And every year new Christmas items appear in the stores to catch our fancy, although I have drawn the line at the snoring Santa. Then there are the things you inherit and the things friends and relatives bless you with, and the next thing you know, thirteen large boxes clog your attic!

Christmas tradition at my house when I was growing up meant just that: Christmas was at my house. Everywhere, in every nook and cranny. There wasn't a room or shelf or stair that wasn't laden with or wrapped in or dangled with its presence, and that is what I brought to our marriage.

Most of our closest friends' homes also ooze with Christmas decorations, and it's fun to be a guest, to once again find all their old treasures and spy for new ones. I love Marlene's collection of snowmen and snowwomen. The Ungers have this little Santa that bobs his way down a pole, their whiskered nutcracker, and on the chimney the giant Santa face Barb made so many years ago. Dennis and Judy collect nativity sets, and all the variety reminds me of the many ways Christ will be pictured, in this season, throughout the world and in our hearts.

For the most part, Christmas hurls itself around our homes early and doesn't begin to disappear until some time after New Year's. All except for Mary Beth, who loves the Lord but really doesn't like (gross understatement) the commercial Christmas. Her tree goes up a couple days before Christmas, and on the 26th it's down. Period. And now even that routine has been complicated by a son's asthma. Since the dust mites play havoc with his lungs, she actually has to annually wash her fake tree! Of course she uses Pine Sol for fragrance, but somehow that just isn't the same. This development, I might add, did nothing to endear her any more to the season.

All in all, it's a lot of work, getting all this stuff displayed. When we first bring the booty down, our house looks as if the boxes had upchucked their contents in every direction. There seems to be no way to make this transition without several days of chaos. I have so many rest-of-the-year knickknacks that it gets somewhat tricky putting them away while bringing Christmas out. Trading southwestern pottery for Christmas mice, seashells for Santa soaps, and collector plates propped on the mantel for stockings hanging down—it takes some doing!

61

Dear George never whines about any of this. He faithfully rummages through the attic every year, then repacks it when Christmas is finally sealed back in its boxes. The boxes are my job; carefully nesting delicate objects in tissue doesn't come naturally to George. There has only been one time when he drew the line at a decoration. It was a gift from a friend, a gift that I absolutely adored: a latch-hooked Santa face that went on the toilet lid. (She knows me well.) Now George didn't mind it as a decoration, but in practicality it left something to be desired. The first time George entered the bathroom after I'd decked the john with Santa's beaming face, I heard all this commotion and slamming and banging and thrashing around. It seems the seat wouldn't stay up with all that fluff on the lid, and he was not a happy camper. Santa now grins in someone else's bathroom; I took him to the resale shop.

Of course our decorations wouldn't be complete without mistletoe. What could be more wonderful than a reason to kiss? It hangs from the light fixture in our entryway. No one can pass through our front door and remove their coat without being caught in its magical Smoochville powers. One year I moved it to the top of the doorway above the side entryway into the kitchen. This way I could get George every time he came up out of the garage. And since one of George's nicknames is Garage-man, this turns out to be quite often! Just to throw him off, however, I moved it back to the front door last year. I just think surprises are more fun, don't you?

I used to buy new mistletoe every year, but one year at the tired end of the season I accidentally threw it in the ornament box instead of the garbage, hand-made bow and all. When I discovered it the next year, I gave it a try; much to my surprise, it worked just fine. One less thing to buy.

Yes, I dearly love all our Christmas stuff. But every once in a while I go through a period of wishing we had nothing more than a couple magnificent fresh floral pieces. Tasteful. Elegant. Less work. As I pack our treasures away, however, I look at each of them and find an event or time or person to be thankful for, and I realize that it is worth all the dusting and fussing. The glass snowball with a child and pet inside, given to me by Pat; the music box Al and Barb gave us, with the nativity scene on it, that plays "Silent Night"; the holly teapot and four matching holly cups that were Mom's; the dorky string of green plastic Christmas bells that was about all I could afford the year Bret and I lived by ourselves right after my divorce; an original, decades-old Uncle Mistletoe from Marshall Field's that George's mother gave us, his plaster face now cracking, but oh, what a treasure. The list could go on for pages.

These are pieces of our lives. Each one adds not only to the patchwork of our holidays but to the very core and rhythm of our family. And one day they'll be passed on to our boys, if they're interested.

My most cherished decoration, however, is not something that was handed down. I bought it at least fifteen years ago, and it is the nativity set I mentioned. Actually, it's not the set itself, it is the ritual of unwrapping each piece, arranging them just so—including an angel who hangs high above them—and thinking about that day. The day when Christ was born and shepherds and wise men felt the call.

Joseph, staff in hand, and Mary, eyes full of love, gaze upon their son. How could they ever imagine how that little babe would influence the life of Charlene Ann Baumbich so many centuries later? They are surrounded, in my scene, by goats and sheep and camels, all at peace with one another—a glimpse into the future.

And Jesus, well, unwrapping him from his swaddling of tissue paper always causes my heart to skip a beat. Kneeling on the floor, arranging this scene at the base of a curio cabinet in the entryway, I am struck by the appropriateness of my posture. And in that instant of Christmas chaos, I know that all is well with my soul. All is well.

DAZE SIX

The Lights
(Meltdown)

You'll notice that when I was talking about decorating the tree and the house I never mentioned strings of lights. That's because they are deserving of their own chapter. If ever there was a daze-inducing phenomenon, it is that of putting up the lights and then taking them down again. In fact, we have had—as I'm sure you have had—episodes from which we thought we would never recover, not only emotionally, but literally, as the electrical shock set our hair on end.

My friend told me about a mild-mannered woman she worked with who never raised her voice or got upset. Then one morning she came in livid; it was the second Christmas after her marriage. She was huffing and puffing and carrying on something terrible. My friend asked her what was wrong, and she said, "My husband put the lights away last year, and I assumed he organized them. Well, he didn't! He just took them all down and stuffed them in a bag. They were all so tangled that I had a fit trying to get them apart, and I'm still mad!" Ah, the magic of Christmas.

But what would Christmas be without gabillions of lights? (Aside from less stress.) They are, in some ways, our very image of Christmas. Christmas trees, shrubs, windows, mantels are aglow; trimmed doorways, wreaths and mirrors sparkle and beckon us to gaze and ponder.

Although I'm sure arranging lights has always been a hassle, at least when I was growing up there weren't so many *kinds* to think about. There was a relatively short electrical string, and it came with one of two sizes of bulbs. Now there are minilights and midilights and racing lights and twinkling lights and lights that bubble (my personal favorites). There are lights that sporadically light as certain notes of a song are played, and battery ones for which you don't need an outlet. There are light accessories that cup and cover bulbs. There are ornaments that plug into your light socket and twirl. Strings come in endless lengths and voltages, and finding the appropriate replacement bulb has become a high-tech and time-consuming activity.

Lights hold power. They captivate and mesmerize us; they blow fuses in our homes. They can cause perfectly normal men and women to screech and holler and act generally childish as they battle to unknot, rewind or find the blasted problem with the string—a problem that reveals itself only after it is strung wherever it is going and you've added a layer or two of ornaments and garland. Oh yes, and the bad string is always in the middle of your megastring. And it cannot be brought back to life, no matter how you shake it, replace bulbs, or plug and unplug it. Until you dismantle it and spread it on the floor. Then it works.

Lights, I believe, tell us a lot about the people who hang them. Are they artistic? Are they patient? Are they rich enough to do all the trees in the yard and pay the electric bill? Do they have an engineering degree that enables them to cover all the bushes and still have in hand the wall plug end—one that will actually reach a wall socket?

I remember assembling about eight strings one year. I fussed around and fussed around, plugging strings into one another. Tentacles of lights sprawled in every direction from the abdomen of the energy source, but it had not birthed a dangling end for me to plug them in! I threw the entire wad on the ground and asked George to take over. He is an engineer. Although it did take him a considerable amount of time, his patience was finally rewarded. For this (and for George in general), I am grateful.

And have I mentioned the zillions of extension cords all of this takes?

It is George's duty to assemble our fake tree and "do" the lights. We still use the regular strings (pre-mini), and we enhance them with a few strings of bubblers (flashes of my childhood) and twinklers. As George begins the project, he plugs in each string first to see how many bulbs he has to replace. How they burn out over the summer in our attic is a mystery to me, but they do. And since we have so many twinklers, he has to wait for the lights to warm up, because the twinklers do not twink before their time, and you don't want to throw one away that just wasn't ready yet.

He is not only more patient than I but very good about rearranging via my critique. The only way to tell how they look, if you're putting them on the tree in daylight, is to squint. So he arranges and I squint. I don't know why this works, but it does. Try it sometime.

But even George can come to the end of his rope. When we first bought our house, we were gifted with a blue spruce sapling to plant in the yard. It was so small that George had to put a stake near it to keep from mowing it down. A string of lights would have overwhelmed it and probably cracked its trunk.

Twenty-seven years later, George decided it was time to light it up. He asked me to buy ten strings of lights, and I tried to tell him that wouldn't begin to do it. "We'll see," he said. Right.

Ten strings barely covered the bottom two rounds of this nineteen-foot-base beauty. We bought more strings and more strings, and they still were barely making a dent. So George decided to drape them instead of wind them. It took two clothesline poles taped together and I don't know what else to reach as far as he could, which was still nowhere near the top. After nasty words and burnt strings and watching George crunch bulbs as he stepped on them while trying to circle and drape, I finally surrendered, bowing in honor of the tree's victory. I suspected it was rejoicing in its revenge for the torment and verbal kidding it took as a toddler.

But George, relentlessly pursuing this obsession, drafted our neighbor Linda to help, and the two of them were out there for hours, grumbling and laughing. Finally they called it quits when they had again run out of lights and used up every implement available in an attempt to reach farther than humanly possible. Even George had run out of patience.

We were the only people in our neighborhood who had a two-thirds decorated tree. It was beautiful. As long as you drove by at night, you didn't know how far the lights were from the top. And they glowed with silent dignity, as opposed to some trees that flash and twinkle and shine, all at the same time. (Honestly, you expect disco music to blare from the roots at any moment! But then, that's what floats their boat, so who are we to complain?)

Complain? Yes, there are several stories each year on the news concerning neighborhood light complaints. It seems some people get carried away: they illuminate not only their yard but the sky for blocks around, which is what the neighbors complain about. That and the fact they cannot even get into their own neighborhood at night for the traffic jam caused by sightseers drawn to the lights.

* * *

Hmmm. Drawn to the lights. Drawn to the Light. Is that what we're instinctively doing with all our lights, even though we are not cognitively aware of it? Could it be that our spirits are quietly trying to pull us in the right direction, toward the Light of the Christ Child?

"Be a star and poke a hole in someone's darkness." I read

that once. And it is the light of the Lord that has illuminated our darkness, once and for all. May we remember that with every socket, string, tangle and bulb.

DAZE SEVEN

The Crafts
(Adventure Land)

Everyone loves crafts.

Okay, some of us like doing them, and some of us just like buying them.

I like both. At Christmas time, fruits of my craftmaking, as well as those of the boys as they were growing up, are sprinkled everywhere in our house. Each represents a phase of our lives.

My love for crafting has ebbed and flowed throughout my life, as most things do. Although I vaguely remember as a kid getting involved with those potholders you make on a little loom, the first *real* craft I knew how to do was crochet. I was visiting a cabin on a lake with some friends of my parents, and Helen taught me how to crochet doilies. I learned that I didn't have much use for doilies but that I did like to crochet.

Although I didn't spend a lot of time throughout my childhood years crocheting, the skill stayed with me. As I grew into adulthood, crocheted Christmas presents began to make their way into the lives of some of my relatives. I once made my mother a gold sweater out of modified granny squares. (Don't even think about how much courage it took for her to actually wear it.) I crocheted Grandma and Aunt Del each a nifty little fold-over sewing kit. The pattern came from one of those women's magazines that always hit the market in late summer and early fall with all kinds of money-saving ideas for crafty gifts you can make. These are the magazines that are difficult to throw away. I still have some from the seventies, in a drawer in my craft dresser in the basement—where I have sadly discovered the mice are running a colorful B&B!

I crocheted a baby blanket over the holidays while I was waiting for Brian to arrive; he was born December 30. It was pink and blue and white and obviously before ultrasound. I was glad I had something calming to do on the outside because he was trying to crack ribs from the inside.

One time I crocheted a Santa Claus, face and all. He was about a foot tall and had a removable hat. It wasn't until I got him all stuffed and sewn up that I realized I hadn't put enough batting in; his head flopped forward and he became the perpetual navel-gazing Santa. I finally gave him away last year, after asking my boys if they were interested. They might have been if he'd been around when they were younger, but he was too new to have old memories.

When I was pregnant with Bret I took a knitting class. Now keep in mind I was only nineteen years old and didn't really have a clue about how long it would take to knit a sweater. In fact, I didn't have a clue about a lot of things, but that's another book. At any rate, I was so excited about my class that I bought four sweater kits when the store from which I was taking the class ran a yarn sale. Wouldn't Christmas be special when I delivered these gifts knitted and purled with my own little fingers?

Every once in a while Dad reminds me about the half of a sweater front and bagful of yarn he received, with my promise to complete the job. I never did. Truth was, I hated knitting.

I went through a needlepoint phase. Made Mom an eyeglass holder, whipped up a few small picture-type things, then spent over 500 hours (yes, I logged them) on this blooming cactus of a wall hanging. I was never so glad to be done with anything in my life. My mom thought it was beautiful, but then she thought everything I made was beautiful, even when it wasn't. I haven't needlepointed since, although I did enjoy that more than knitting.

After the kids were born, it was fun to do crafts with them, especially Christmas crafts that kept their little "Boy, am I excited about Christmas!" energies busy with something productive. Our tree is laced with evidence of the Christmas we made Shrinky Dinks, and the year we painted little wooden ornaments, and the year we made dough people. Brian made a most excellent Mr. Bill. Remember him? "Oh No-o-o-o-o." I love hanging him near the trunk (fake trunk now, of course) in a spot where he kind of peeks through the branches and spies on us.

We had such a good time with that dough that I got a little carried away with my goals and decided to make a nativity scene. Well, the three main characters. Just try to picture Joseph with hair made of dough squished through a garlic press, and Mary with eyes too wide for her head, and baby Jesus, who looked more like an old wooden clothespin than a child. Brian set it up in his room for a couple years, but the entire family started crumbling. So much for holiness through dough art!

One year we got excited about pinning sequins into styrofoam. And when the boys were really little, of course they glued macaroni to cardboard, then painted it gold. Didn't we all? But the most creative and fun ornament project was the year we made soft-sculpture faces. It was also the last craft project we did together, since the boys were verging on being too old to "do crafts" with Mom. I made a couple of these things, and then they wanted to try it too. We gathered around a table full of old nylons and needles and thread and bits of batting and red material. The variety and ingenuity was a thing to behold! And laughter was plentiful as we pulled the thread through the backs of these heads, creating sideways grins and inverted noses. Men, women, kids, Santa, glasses, beards, dimples. Each year when I'm opening tree-decoration boxes, I am always filled with joy when I open the lid and rediscover those faces staring up at me. It's not just the faces that give me a grin; it's the memory of time spent together, crafting, sharing, laughing and learning little things about one another. All worth the huge mess we made (which is also still etched in my memory).

I have a collection of Christmas mice; my favorite is about eight inches tall and her body is made out of a gray sock. She has button eyes and yarn whiskers, and she's wearing a holiday hat and apron. She has a wonderfully long felt tail that I get a kick out of arranging just so, when I decide where to showcase her for the season. But my favorite thing about her is that she was made by my friend Mary Gingell and shipped all the way from Oregon. I can still hear Mary's laughter during my "Merry

Christmas and thank you" phone call, when she told me how many times she'd redone the eyes and whiskers to keep poor Mrs. Mouse from looking demented. Our friendship spans a quarter of a century now, and this is the precious stuff it is made of. Laughter. Conversation. Child-rearing horrors and stories. Careers that blossomed after child-rearing. Menopause. A mouse made of a sock.

From the time I was in sixth grade, I bowled every year in a league. In fact, I was third-highest female junior bowler in the state of Illinois in 1963, the year I graduated from high school. As an adult, I bowled in a scratch league, and some of the women I competed against had been my coaches throughout the years. What a cycle.

I finally had to give up bowling due to chronic sciatica problems. But I am reminded with great fondness about some of those people when I decorate my tree, because many of my ornaments were handcrafted by women who drew my name in the gift exchange for the annual Christmas party. Although any gift can mark time, there is something about a handmade gift made especially for you that cloaks it in undying warmth. A gift that someone created bit by bit.

Working with your hands on something creative gives your brain a rest from worries. It sets a pace that slows you down to one stitch at a time. One thought at a time. One moment in time—a moment that is a small piece of the bigger picture. It is often not until we do slow down that we realize how fast we were going. Rushing. Buying. Shopping. Planning. Whisking right past the point of the season.

Lord, help me remember to pace myself one stitch at a time this holiday season, and to make you the canvas to which I sew the pieces of my heart.

DAZE EIGHT

The Cards
(Fantasy Land)

October 30. I must be the most clever person on earth. Here it is the day before Halloween, and I have already purchased my Christmas stamps! Never mind that I haven't stocked our cupboards with Halloween candy yet; the Christmas stamps are in my possession.

Yes, this is one baby step toward an antistress Christmas

year. No waiting in massive holiday postal lines for me; no grumbling about slow counter personnel.

I have no shame: I've told everyone I ran into today, whether I knew them or not, that, yessiree-bob, I have my Christmas stamps right here in my handbag. (This said while stroking leather, smiling like a two-year-old who just pooped his pants and seems proud of it. Right.)

Not only do I have the stamps, but I bought my Christmas cards last year during the post-Christmas holiday sales. And I even know where they are. They're in our bedroom in the bag with last year's Christmas cards we received. Cards that I want to go through just one last time before I chuck them. My intentions were to do this before we took the tree down. So much for bragging.

This one-last-time scenario is something I've been doing for years. So often the cards are read in such a passing frenzy that news doesn't have a chance to soak in. I like to read the verses, *really* read the verses, in an unhurried manner, allowing them to minister to me. I like to make a deliberate study of the looks on the children's faces in any photographs that might have been enclosed. I like to sometimes write letters of response. I like to find forgotten checks or dollar bills.

I always used to predict the two to five dollars that would fall out of Grandma's card. Something for "yous to split. Not much, but mayby get an ice cream cone." When I was growing up, Dad used to tongue-in-cheek refer to Grandma's letters as "another *Life Can Be Beautiful* from the Bluejay."

"Dearest ones," she always began, "Hope yous are all fine." Then there would be a litany of several pages detailing each and every ailment with which she and everyone she knew suffered. Who had died. Who was in a nursing home. Always particulars about weather conditions. "Love, Mom."

Grandma never attended high school, and her spelling was even worse than mine. We all got a good chuckle the year she'd been to Dallas, Texas, and wrote to tell us about the "buteifull sky crapper buildings" she'd seen.

Yes, the dollar or two from Grandma meant a lot. And we did get ice cream. And I miss her funny, silly, loving cards and letters. I miss her.

This one last reading of the cards is a time to be thankful not only for those cards we received, but for the people in our lives who cared enough about us to send them. For those who no longer are able to send cards, for whatever reasons, but who have blessed our lives in countless ways. For the body of friends and family that surrounds us during the holiday season—even when it seems to be pressing in a little too closely during those last-minute buying crusades.

*   *   *

November 29. Thanksgiving is behind us. Time to do the cards. Wouldn't it be something if I actually beat the usual early birds?

*   *   *

Can't believe it's December 14 already! Honestly, where does time go? Here I have the Christmas packages ready for UPS, and my cards aren't even started! Maybe this should be the year I write one of those Xeroxed Christmas letters. I know some people whine about them; some are even offended. But we learn more in those letters than we do from a couple of speedily hand-scrawled lines on a card. These days, sometimes the entire card seems computer generated.

Computer labels on the envelope. Preprinted names on the card. No "Hi" or anything. Not even a personal ink spot. I'd much rather receive a "hi, everyone" letter; at least you learn *something* about your friends' lives, even if it's just that your own life is as boring as canned peas compared to some of theirs.

Actually, we've indulged in our own brand of personal Christmas communications. In fact, I wish I'd kept one of each of the cards we've sent over our years of marriage. It would probably reflect more of our lives than we could imagine.

When the children were young, beautiful Santas were popular every couple years. We went through a spell of having to have four snowmen, or four whatever, because that's how many *we* were. Then there were times when I felt a need to convey a specific message, and the verse became of far greater importance than the mood of the art work. The year Mom died, I wrote a poem and had it printed on nice, heavy paper. Later I went through a sparkly stage. Whatever glittered.

And now, we pick what we like based on the following criterion: It's on sale. George would like to retire one day.

*   *   *

It's December 18 and I've decided that Christmas cards are a waste of time. Just one more thing I don't have a minute to do. Just one more way for retailers to yank us around, for the United States Postal Service to get rich. Another pressure and stress builder. Why bother? Why make myself crazy and stay up late and get crabby and complain and . . .

Everybody deserves one year when they choose not to do cards. I mean, who's patting my back with congratulations that I've never once even been tardy with cards before? Nobody.

I once read a story wherein the writer said her family decided every year to skip one piece of commercial Christmas. Maybe the cards, or the wrapping, or a gift exchange. I hereby adopt that policy and choose cards!

*   *   *

Just about the time doing cards seems like nothing more than a greeting-card-manufacturers' gimmick and simply one more thing to check off my Christmas marathon list, I do receive a note in someone's card. A cherished line that rings my Christmas bells and vibrates the strings of my heart.

Perhaps it isn't the doing of the cards that needs to be considered. Perhaps it is the motives for doing the cards that we must annually examine. Am I just checking someone off my list, or am I checking on them? Am I duty-bound or mission-oriented? Am I in holiday-reflex mode, or heart-motivated?

We truly *do* remember and often talk about many friends throughout the year, and I want them to know we remember them, don't I? I want them to be as happy to hear from us as we are to know they still miss our gatherings. Think about us. A quick "Remember when . . ." that causes memories of Christmases past to march by in warm details. Messages of intent to "get together some time," which we always mean but don't always act on. References to inside jokes that no one but us would get.

There is something about gazing upon the Christ Child's serene face in my snow-white, glazed, ceramic nativity set that compels me, beckons me, to smile upon others. No, the torqued-up face of a harried salesperson isn't the face of Christmas. Cards shouldn't be a duty. Cards present an opportunity to reflect on blessings, to pass on the peace and love in the smile of the Christ Child.

My favorite experiences doing cards have been when I've set several hours aside to indulge in relationships rather than simply chalk something up as done. I get out my Christmas stamps. Light a fragrant candle and bring a steeping cup of tea laced with cinnamon to my work place. Say a prayer of thanksgiving for the blessing of each person, couple and family who have touched our lives.

Cards. What a wonderful opportunity for praise and thanksgiving.

*   *   *

'Twas two days before Christmas
and all through the house
not a creature was stirring
'cuz we were waiting
for Wonderdog Butch to hurl
as he'd gotten into (and eaten)
an entire box of
Frango Mints he found under the tree!

This is the opening *true* story—and exact date of writing—for my First Annual Christmas Letter. You know what they say about best-laid plans, as well as what Scripture tells us about pride going before a fall. (Why, oh why, was I so smug about my stamps?) Three snappy, succinct paragraphs about our lives follow my poem. (I use that word very loosely.) I sign off: "Peace (and grins) on earth. Good will toward everyone. May you be showered with grace and blessings—just when you need a refreshing lift. Relax: God is in the director's chair. Happy New Year."

*   *   *

Two days after Christmas, and for the first time in my adult life, I didn't get Christmas cards mailed. I even paid to have photocopies of my First Annual Christmas Letter printed, and I never mailed them. They're in the bag with last year's cards we received and I haven't gone through one last time yet, cards I bought last year to mail this year, and the stamps I purchased before Halloween. Wouldn't you know, this is the year stamps are going up in price as of January 1, and my ain't-I-something October purchase won't be worth squat if I don't get these in the mail. So what if they're a little late?

* * *

February 27. I'm still paying bills and writing letters that are being mailed with two stamps: one Santa, one blue bird. The Christmas bag and all its contents remain untouched. Guess next year I'll type Annual Letter Number Two and begin it with, "P.S. Wonderdog Butch never did hurl. Another Christmas miracle!" I'll simply staple this year's letter to it so they'll know what I'm talking about and I won't have wasted copy money.

In the meantime, I shall give thanks to God who sent his only Son to be born, and die, and rise from the dead, all because we could never be perfect.

It isn't the cards that matter. It's Jesus. Let me remember to write that in my cards, all throughout the year. And I thank God for sending him to us. No buying, mailing or stamping necessary. Just an "I believe" and he's yours. Forever.

DAZE NINE

The Shopping (Survival)

I could open this chapter with one word: *shopping*. Everyone would know what daze I was talking about. You could each add your own personal sound effect: a sigh, groan, stomp of your foot or crabby phrase. I could leave a blank page and give you time to stare into it before your next bout of shopping. Kind of a resting place. In fact, that's such a brilliant idea, I'm gonna do it!

Shopping

Now that we're somewhat refreshed after our pause for the cause (revisit that page whenever you feel a need for a moment of nothingness), let's carry on with what is one of the dizziest dazes of the holiday season. This is where our lists come into speed-of-light play, whipping in and out of our pockets and handbags—as does our money, except that the money whips permanently out.

This is where our crafting swings into high gear if we've lots of supplies to buy. This is where wonder turns to wilt and the dream takes a wrong turn and traditions are questioned—especially the buying of gifts—and the tree is of little importance if there's nothing to put under it, and there's probably something on your shopping list that you need to finish your decorating and . . .

You get the picture: All elements run at high speed and hold the potential to go careening down the slippery slope into Scroogeville, when Christmas Shopping is hanging over your head.

Except for my friend Judy, who loves to shop. Every weekend. All year round. Doesn't miss a giant craft fair, doesn't miss a sale, doesn't lose her smile, even though she works full time. She has endless energy and patience for the Christmas Shopping Season, and I wish I could borrow it.

She even flew from Chicago to Minneapolis for a day-long shopping trip at the Mall of America—alone. She couldn't find anyone else to go with her. She said she did it "all" that day, including riding the Ferris wheel (for those not in the know, there's an entire amusement park plus billions of stores and restaurants in this megamall) so she could see from the tippy top. She wants everyone to be wowed Christmas morning, and she spends the entire year looking for those special things that cause people to say, "Where in the world did you find this? How did you know I'd love this? I've *never* seen one of these before." She loves, loves, loves Christmas shopping, causing me to wonder if I'm missing something. But I doubt it.

As my crafting bouts ebb and flow, so does my approach to shopping. It wasn't until a few years ago that, for the most part, I had all my shopping to do between Thanksgiving and Christmas. (Okay, it was more like the two weeks before Christmas and it was the king of all beat-the-clock endeavors.)

Then one year something inside me went *sproing!* (probably the beginning of my hormonal rushes), and since it twanged, I have become obsessed with getting my shopping done before Thanksgiving, so I can have the month of December to be more relaxed about the tree, decorating, cards, baking, entertaining. Funny thing is, the two weeks before Thanksgiving, I'm completely harried trying to beat my own deadline. I do not circumvent the crazies; I simply have moved the timeline to one that doesn't feel so crowded.

There are pros and cons to both early and late shopping. Putting all the shopping off until December has an obvious flaw: that's when everything else needs to get done and stores are out of all the cool, popular stuff. However, markdown sales are ripe. Unfortunately, so are many of the people with whom you will be smashed into elevators and lines because we've been sweating, lugging giant shopping bags around which have caused our fingers and arms to go numb, and we are too intent on getting our shopping done to take our coats off (also, we'd need to sprout a third arm to carry them), and our body temperatures are causing us to cook in our own toxins.

On the other hand, although a condensed late-shopping time does have its stresses, it also has a perk: the agony only lasts a short while.

Shopping early is nice because, well, you're done early. However, I find it's easy to spend more money this way. You say you're "Done!" but trendy new items keep coming out and you decide to add just this one more thing. About twelve times.

When you ask people in October to tell you what they want for Christmas, they just can't think about it that early, so you decide for them. Then they spring to life in December and give you a call and tell you the item that is all, *all,* they want—which is not what you got them. Now you're left with the struggle: Do you return what you bought and replace it with what they want, or just give them both? Or do you make them suffer by ignoring their tardy request because they wouldn't oblige you in October? Didn't take you seriously because of your last-minute-shopping track record.

No matter when you do your shopping, one thing is certain: We are all going too fast these days, so not too many people harbor reserve energies to be shopping with a perky face, aside from Judy. Thus, we have no patience. Thus, we are fraught with short fuses. Thus, shopping malls are like an overloaded switch box that's ready to blow. Kids are whining and want to ride the little trains that go in circles, which is where you feel like you're going with your lists.

What are all these scillion crazed people doing in this mall breathing my air?

*   *   *

Sometimes we need to snatch a leisurely "fun" shopping excursion that doesn't have much pressure, like the one my friend Mar and I took several years ago. Once a year I like to take the train downtown—Chicago downtown, Loop downtown, scary downtown if you're from the "burbs"—to see the Chicago Christmas sights. Animated windows, decorated buildings, people singing on street corners, chestnuts roasting in a barrel and for sale by the bag to eat on the spot, and the giant tree in Marshall Field's (shades of yesteryear). Oh yes, and beggars and homeless people and people with purple hair singing very bad songs I never heard of.

It is an excursion that makes me celebrate that the kid in

me is alive and well and full of wonder, and a day that chagrins the adult in me, who can be terrorized by listening to the other adult I live with as he gives me twenty-seven warnings about pickpockets, rapists and every other horrible act of humankind he can think of.

Mar and I had pretty much decided to ride the 9:26 from Glen Ellyn, but as things often go with us, we actually rode the 10:26. I was glad a time clock wasn't waiting on the other end of the line. And glad our church was right next to the Glen Ellyn train station so we could secure a last-minute parking space; otherwise we might not have arrived in Chicago until the stores closed. (Who says it doesn't pay to be a Christian?!)

We found we were not going to be "doing Chicago" alone. The suburban station was buzzing with would-be shoppers, part of the late-morning working force and others who would be departing the train somewhere between here and the Loop.

We purchased our round-trip tickets and waited for the bells to start dinging. Within minutes we were on our way.

We were unable to find two seats together. I ended up seated next to a serious commuter—the kind wearing a two-piece suit, black nylons and Adidas, reading the *Wall Street Journal* before hauling a giant wad of documents out of her briefcase.

"Something going on downtown today?" she asked, eyeing all the chattering ladies.

"Just Christmas shopping, as far as I know," I responded.

"Oh, yeah," she said. "All the nonworking people."

This journey took place several years ago; I was still full-time mothering. *If she thinks that's not work* . . . The hair on my neck stood up. This statement goes directly to the button in my brain that engages *Warning: you are being attacked. All motherhood is being attacked. Rise to your own defense and that of all mothers!* But I squelched my spiteful retort behind a smile. After all, this was a *fun* day, and no one was going to spoil it.

"Fa la la la la, la la la la," I sang to myself.

I also tucked my purse more securely under my arm. After all, this might be a sneak attack by a perverted thief to distract my attention. George's darker worries surfaced in my brain.

"We must be annoying," I suddenly found myself saying to *her* at the end of my inner muttering.

"Who?"

"Us. The ones who break your routine. The chatty ones. Who might unknowingly take one of your 'reserved' seats you sit in every day. The ones who do nothing but give our full attention to raising tomorrow's leaders."

Silence.

"I don't always take this train," she said defensively. It was her turn to scramble.

Good. We were on a defensive par.

I should have been kinder, filled with Christmas spirit. I'll admit I failed in that. I leaned across the aisle and chatted with Mar, laughing uproariously—and a little too loudly—all the way to Chicago.

Our day lived up to its expectations. Lunch was wonderful. We didn't get lost. I came home with my purse, an overstuffed shopping bag, caramel corn and a lot less money than I had left with. We had seen the sights: animated windows, decorated buildings, people singing on street corners, chestnuts roasting in a barrel and the giant tree in Marshall Field's—along with homeless people sitting on the sidewalks talking to themselves.

We even managed to catch the express train home. Of course

that wasn't much of a task, because as soon as you head in the direction of the train station during rush hour, the current of the people will carry you there, like a horse heading for the barn, even if that's not where you want to go.

We survived our excursion. As for the businesswoman on the train, it never hurts to have your values challenged, for that is often when we find out what we're *really* thinking—and have the spontaneous boldness to let others know about it.

*   *   *

Finally comes the moment when you realize your shopping is done. What a relief!

And it lasts for about two seconds. Then you remember you now have to wrap everything, maybe mail it someplace, maybe even overnight it, depending on your timeline.

Wrapping. Kind of its own sub-daze category. Used to be, since I didn't get my shopping done until the last minute, wrapping was a Christmas Eve nightmare. I'd have to wait until the kids went to bed and I thought they were sleeping; then George would help me haul the stuff from the car trunk, the basement, under the bed, my underwear drawer—wherever I could stuff, stash or cram it when no one was looking. We'd drag all the wrapping goodies out and begin. Keep in mind, I'm not good when I'm tired. In fact, I'm very bad. And getting ready to wrap late Christmas Eve is about as bad as it gets, for obvious reasons.

George would always offer to help, which I would accept. That's where the plan would crack: it was the first time he saw the price tags. Grumbling would turn to sniping until finally I delivered my diatribe.

"I have to do everything, blah blah blah . . . maybe you'd like to do all the Christmas shopping next year, blah blah . . ." And then I'd be afraid he'd say yes to that (which he would have, because he is always ready to help when I ask, and often when I don't), so I'd shut up and proceed to wrap in a snit, knowing my procrastination and martyrism were doing me in. He'd finally storm off to bed leaving me alone, which I deserved. (And I hate it when it's my fault, especially when I'm already mad.)

Time would drag on as I wrapped; grumbling and often tears stained the holy night; morning drew near as I finally staggered down and tucked all the packages under the tree; the kids woke up before dawn and immediately after I went to bed. Ditto for several years in a row.

Merry Christmas. This is not how Christ hopes we remember his birth.

*   *   *

Do not be afraid. I bring you good news of great joy that will be for all the people. Today in the town of David a Savior has been born to you; he is Christ the Lord. (Luke 2:10-11)

For God so loved the world that he gave his one and only Son, that whoever believes in him shall not perish but have eternal life. (John 3:16)

Mary treasured up all these things and pondered them in her heart. The shepherds returned, glorifying and praising God for all the things they had heard and seen, which were just as they had been told. (Luke 2:19-20)

Lord, save me from making a mockery out of your great love and sacrifice for me. Cause your Word to vibrate in my heart when

I forget why we call this Christ-mas.

Help my spirit of giving be filled with your Spirit of mercy and love for my family and friends. Stop me from judging strangers on trains and street corners, with their own stresses and maybe even purple hair. Save me from greed and commercialism—and from the sin of ever seeing any of your precious children as simply one more person to buy for, then cross off our lists.

Empower me to recognize what doesn't need to be done, and give me the good grace to let go of it. Help me remember as I shop and wrap that you are watching me make the choices.

When I encounter a crabby salesperson or cranky child, may your light shine through my responses. When I look in the mirror and see my own frazzled self, may I remember to look to you, from whom my strength and refreshment comes.

Help me to remember what you have already done in my life, for it is in studying your sovereignty, not in buying worldly possessions, that I will find peace and joy and truth.

DAZE TEN

The Cooking (Dough, Dips and Disasters)

L et me begin this chapter by saying that I believe in the mystical, magical Christmas powers of a box of Oreo cookies and those ginger-snappery Jingles that are covered with holiday sparkles. Yes, a frozen pizza or a roll of store-bought cookie dough baked in your own oven is about as homemade as it gets, some years. The only way to beat some of the dazes is to be good stewards of our time, and sometimes it's the excess kitchen duty that needs to go. We should not feel guilty about keeping our local bakeries in business. After all, bakers need to feed their families too.

And don't forget Mary and Martha. Although Martha felt it her duty to be slaving (and perhaps feeling martyrish) in the kitchen, it was Mary who was sitting at the feet of Christ, listening to his stories, winning his praises for drawing near. If only they'd had Oreo cookies and frozen pizza in those days, perhaps Martha would have made a better choice.

But whose holiday traditions and celebrations don't conjure up images of food? Crowded tables? Traditional dishes? Over-flowing cookie jars? Hors d'oeuvres? Candy? Mmmmm.

I once read an article that proclaimed how much weight the average person gains over the holidays, and I'm here to tell you, if you don't gain, I know where your deficient share on the "average" charts ends up; I'm sitting on it.

Christmas memories can be brought to life for me any time of year by the wafting scent of gingerbread. Salivary glands spring into action as I imagine the pineapple cream filling of my mom's pie sliding across the roof of my mouth as I close it around the fork and rake the delicacy off the tines, leaving the precious gold, for just a moment, filling my entire oral cavity with excitement. I can seem to feel the sugary coating of sprinkles pass my lips as I dream of chomping down on a warm cut-out cookie.

I can see raw egg noodles draped here, there and everywhere as the limp homemade dough dries in preparation for boiling in the giblet juices, soon to be poured over the top of steaming, freshly mashed potatoes. (Yes, my family puts noodles on potatoes.)

More important than the food itself is the gathering around it. The Spirit among us who stirs the ingredients of our hearts, beckons and soothes our psyches. The coming together of family and friends for the purpose of fellowship—and pigging out. Yea, Christmas!

When the boys were little, I had an unwritten motto: Bake without ceasing. (I'm lucky to get one batch out now.) We had cut-out cookies, candy-cane cookies, almond-roll cookies, chowmein-noodle cookies with chocolate and raisins, kolache, spice bread . . .

One year I used eight large Tupperware bowls storing the dozens of baked goods we churned out (and thoroughly trashed the kitchen making). It was fun preparing plates of sweets to take to parties or give to friends. Friends who baked just as many cookies as I, but happily accepted them anyway, as did I theirs. No wonder it seemed the holidays raced by: We were all on relentless sugar highs.

Then my friend Jo taught me how to make crack candy, and that became an annual tradition. We'd boil the sugar concoction, add the flavor oils, pour it in buttered pans and wait. When the consistency was just right, we'd whack away at it, breaking it into bite-size pieces.

It reminded me of making popcorn balls at Grandma's when I was a young'un. All that waiting while Grandma poured drips of the boiling goo into a glass to test for the soft-ball stage (or was it hard-ball?). We'd stand breathlessly as she fished the drop out of the bottom of the glass and rolled it between her fingers. Sometimes we'd have to wait through several torturous rounds of this before she'd finally pop the little round wad in her mouth, smile and declare, "It's ready!" Then she'd pour the delicious brown stream out of her large pan and drizzle it onto the larger bowl of waiting popcorn. Brother Jimmy, cousin J. R. and I would slip our hands through the plate of butter, gurshing and smacking them around, threatening to grab each other's faces. Then we'd make the most wonderful popcorn balls this side of heaven. Boy, what fun.

My boys and I pulled taffy a couple years. My sister-in-law taught us that aerobic art. Unfortunately, getting the taffy mixture to the just-right stage was not my gift, and we threw away several batches as well as the short-lived tradition itself.

Bar none, however, the annual favorite was cut-out cookies with Mom's recipe. What a mess we made, but oh, what memories—from my childhood and parenting days! The boys could each invite a friend, and there is no limit to the imagination of kids turned loose with a pile of cookie cutters, sprinkles, paint brushes and egg yolks with food dye. If you don't believe me, and even if you don't have kids, invite some over. It was always good to have more hands than less, because eventually the novelty wore off, and if it was just the two of them, I'd turn my back for a moment and whirl around to find twelve cookies piled with whatever handful of stuff they'd grabbed, just to be done.

After they were in their teens, I tried to resurrect the cookie-decorating party one last time. Brian's friend Bob, who had been around for many of the Christmas-past decorating parties, happened to be present this day, as did Bret's friend Paul. They didn't seem to be having that good a time, but they were making their best effort to humor Mom, who was so excited about trying to relive an old tradition.

Suddenly their heads were together, huddled over the table so I couldn't see what they were doing. They were laughing. Man, were they laughing! Finally, the unveiling. They'd mixed all the paint colors together, creating this very dark and horrid hue. Then they, ahem, somewhat modified an old standard. They were very proud to present to me—ta dah—the angel of death!

Boys. I knew it was time to throw in the towel on this tradition.

One of my biggest rewards from enduring all the messes is finding that my grown boys like to cook. Never mind that I occasionally get a call asking, "Mom, what does bad hamburger *really* smell like?" (yes, I do lose sleep over questions like that); I am delighted to field their questions and pass on recipes. Fact of the matter is, Bret could outcook me any day. He is Mr. Gourmet and doesn't really like fast-food restaurants, which to me are one of the basic food groups. He collects cookbooks and grinds some of his own spices. And Brian made an entire Thanksgiving dinner for a friend last year, homemade sweet-potato dish and all.

There are recipes I make again and again for holiday gatherings and events during the year, and they include Judy Smith's Sloppy Joes, Robbie Davenport's Creamed Carrots and Onions (also her Grated Potato Casserole), Barb Unger's Pizza Things, Mary Gingell's Crab Foo Young, Hazel Smith's Pineapple Cheese Ball, Kay Carlson's Shrimp Mousse, Marlene Fenske's Whiskied Weenies, Shirley Harvey's Potato Salad Secret and Johanna Flaherty's Carrot Cake, to name a few. And now my boys ask for those recipes, and they write them all down as

Mom's Whatever, because I'm the vehicle through which they learned about them.

Bret and I were talking one day about how recipes become Somebody's. I said, "Won't it be fun when your kids ask for Grandma's Whatever recipe one day?" And he said, "No, Mom, I'll cook it for them, so they'll be asking for Dad's Whatever, because to them, that's whose it will be." Yes, son. Yes, sons. That is my dream for both of you.

What beauty there is in tradition passed on through the lively art of food. What joy there is in breaking bread together and sharing our stories. What a gift it is to be in possession of hand-written recipes, especially those that are layered with spills and spatters—signs of something well tried and shared.

I have wept at estate sales when I find a cookbook packed with hand-written recipes from Aunt Mabel and Sister Susie and Cousin Alice that have come to the end of the line in a family. I have wept over the fact I never found my mom's recipe for what she called "My Man's Cookies."

But I spend more time giving thanks for the hands that

prepare and the hearts that care, and yes, even the messes. "Thank God for dirty dishes, they have a tale to tell. While others may go hungry, we're eating very well." So reads an old spoon rest I bought years ago. Its handle is broken and the body is chipped, but it is part of my kitchen treasures and a potent message to ponder on grumbling days.

Yet there's always room for new recipes, and about five years ago I found a holiday recipe about as outrageous as they get: stuffing the Christmas turkey with dressing made out of White Castle hamburgers (lovingly referred to as "sliders" because they slide down easily). In fact, White Castle hamburgers are such a favorite around here that George and I had them for breakfast on New Year's Day to get the year started on the right foot. With a love like this, how could I pass up the opportunity to stuff the turkey with them?

I told my family what I was doing, and they all thought it was wonderful. (Our boys are as addicted as we are. Santa brings them White Castle gift certificates every year so they can pound a few down while they're in town.)

With great glee I served The Dressing to our little family plus

George's brother's family of four and Grandma and Grandpa Baumbich. Mum was the word about its ingredients.

About halfway through dinner Grandma Baumbich said, "This dressing is so good. What kind of meat is in it?"

I began laughing so hard that I could barely talk. So did the rest of my family. "It's made with White Castle hamburgers!" I finally croaked out. Thekla, my sister-in-law, said, "I saw that recipe in the newspaper, but I said to myself, 'Who would dare try *that?*'"

By consensus, at the Baumbich household, it was declared wonderful! Basically, the dressing is made of ripped-up White Castle burgers—*sans* the pickles—plus some broth, spices and celery.

In case you'd like to add this recipe to your beloved family cookbook, the official White Castle recipe follows (as well as another "special" recipe). They also have lots of other cool recipes made with sliders; you might want to ask for copies during your next visit to the Castle.

What, I wonder, will the heading at the top of my boys' recipe cards one day say about this one?

White Castle ® Turkey Stuffing

Ingredients:

10 White Castle hamburgers, with pickle removed
1½ cups celery, diced
1¼ tsp. ground thyme
1½ tsp. ground sage
¾ tsp. coarse ground black pepper
¼ cup chicken broth

In a large mixing bowl, tear the White Castle hamburgers into pieces and add diced celery and seasonings. Toss and add chicken broth. Toss well. Stuff cavity of turkey just before roasting.

Note: Allow 1 White Castle hamburger for each pound of turkey, which will be equivalent to ¾ cup of stuffing per pound.
Makes about 9 cups (enough for a 10-12 lb. turkey).

Note: Charlene adds one diced apple to this recipe. It's a family tradition.

Recipe copyrighted by and reprinted with permission from White Castle, Inc., 555 W. Goodale St., Columbus, Ohio 43215-1158.

The Angel of Death Cookie

Ingredients:

1 lump cookie dough, flattened
1 angel cookie cutter
Sprinkles
Frostings tinted with various colors of food coloring
2 or more creative kids
Sense of humor

Mix all frostings and sprinkles together until mixture turns a yucky shade of brownish gray. Cut angel with cutter, using warm dough so it sticks to table and when you try to lift it off it stretches into grotesque shape. Let kids add toppings; give them enough free rein to do what comes naturally, thereby causing you to wonder who their *real* parents are. Try not to become hysterical; this is the stuff memories are made of.

Bake at 350° (or thereabouts) until edges are black, giving the already horrid cookie an aura of darkness and a burnt smell.

Recipe copyrighted by no one at all; full credit should be given to Bret, Brian and friends.

DAZE ELEVEN

The Entertaining
(Don't Use the
Guest Towels!)

After much debating and to and fro-ing and contemplating our busy lives, George and I decide it is time for another Christmas open house. We scan our chaotic calendar and discover that there is one possible date before Christmas, so we settle on it. Several years have passed since last we were struck with this terrific idea (takes a while to recuperate at our age), and it seems far too long since we've seen some of our friends. Although life is terribly hectic—and for a moment, several moments, we almost change our minds again—we forge ahead.

I mine every Tupperware party list and personal phone book I own, to make sure I don't miss someone. We decide to mix and match from many of our groups of friends: oldies, newbies, professional—and especially the funsters!

The keys on my computer keyboard blaze as I whip up a lively invitation announcing snacks, beverages and fellowship, make a few phone calls—since I am busting with enthusiasm—and begin my grocery list. This list is comprised of ingredients for my "usual" fare, which is everybody else's recipes, which I've already talked about, plus my ever-popular garlic dip (blend with mixer 8 oz. cream cheese, 1 giant clove fresh garlic, crushed, and enough milk to soften for dipping).

Having this open house is also an opportunity (and justification for its purchase) to use the cute set of cutout things that I bought at the Milwaukee Fair several decades ago after watching the live demonstration. Bologna, bread and mustard can be magically turned into Delicacies-on-a-Toothpick with these multishaped contraptions. There is no limit to the dramatic presentation if you then stick all the food-laden toothpicks into something exotic like an apple. This was done in the live demonstration. With great glee, I add bologna and colored toothpicks to my grocery list in anticipation of such culinary artistry.

As the big day draws near, little bursts of cleaning overtake me. I begin fretting about setting the time for this great event so early in the day. Why would anyone in their right mind invite company while it's still daylight? Everyone knows that when candlelight is your only source of ambience, dust doesn't show! Oh well, there's no way out of it now; guess I'll have to simply clean the corners.

I do a mild amount of grumbling about the oh-so-busy me and revisit the moment in time when we decided to forge ahead instead of bail out. I wonder about my sanity but attach the crevice cleaner to my vacuum and suck cobwebs from around and behind things while I wonder. Honestly, some of these mongo cobwebs are so large, I consider for a moment sprinkling glitter on them. They would be stunning. But alas, good sense wins; I have no glitter and I'm out of time to shop.

For two days, I prepare food.

The morning of the party, I'm down to last-minute details and bathroom cleaning. The timing on bathroom cleaning is everything, especially if you have a man in the house. There is something about the scent of antiseptic cleaners and the lure of the sparkling toilet bowl—not to mention the scoured gleam on your sink—that makes a man want to rub his hands in years-old crank-case oil, then wash them in cold water, scrubbing and splashing and gurshing and squirting grease-laden streams everywhere, then use the guest hand towels with ruffles on the edges.

The fact that I save this task for the last minute, then end up answering the doorbell wearing my rubber gloves, makes George crazy. He just doesn't get it. But he also doesn't take "Do NOT use the guest towels or the bathroom" seriously. You'd think he lived here or something.

Actually we have two bathrooms, but since I'm always cutting my timing so short, I nearly never get to the one upstairs before the doorbell rings. So, as I've told the story elsewhere,

When someone heads that way, I yell, as their foot is mid-way up step two, "No! Use the one down here!"

This is when I unknowingly infringe upon George's space; the space in his brain where he logs items that store up before exploding. One day when we were grumbling about something unrelated to cleaning, George delivered a punch below the belt. He hollered, I mean he *hollered,* "And after 25 years, what do you think people think is *in* that upstairs bathroom!" I have no answer to that, but obviously, I know something George doesn't know: Every household has its room(s) that don't get entered when company comes. Right? (*Mama Said There'd Be Days Like This,* Servant/Vine, p. 94) But this day I actually get to both bathrooms, because the sheer numbers might require that someone ignore my exhortation to stay downstairs. Or, in my whirlwind of hostessing duties, someone might escape.

At any rate, company does begin to arrive, and clean bathrooms and family grumbling are left far behind as kisses under

the mistletoe and firm hugs and welcome greetings and intro-
ductions and conversation bring the house to life with laughter
and joy. For all the trauma, with Christmas shopping and
decorating and lights and on and on ad nauseam, every minute
of torment is worth it as we watch friends gather in our
Christmas House.

Nonstop carols play in the background, thanks to our CD
player; food is eaten and replenished; people come and go. And
there are surprises along the way. Tom and Sue arrive wearing
red Santa hats with fluffy white trim. The tassel on the end of
each of their hats is battery-operated and blinking. Peals of
laughter spread from room to room as they make their way
around our downstairs.

Norman and Maurice arrive, and we're thrilled because we
haven't seen them for a couple years and we had heard they'd
been ill. We have a lovely visit. They are both chipper and
radiant, Norman in his dapper vest, Maurice in her soft pink
sweater adorned with pearls.

*   *   *

Who would know how precious these visits were? We have

since lost our dear friend Tom to cancer. But his grinning, fun-loving presence in our lives will never be forgotten—nor will that shining, blinking Santa-hat entry he made. We thank God for his friendship.

Shockingly, Norman and Maurice died within a short time of one another. A couple, gone.

Lord, help us always to find time in our busy agenda for friends, for we know not what tomorrow brings.

* * *

I'm sitting here looking at a picture from circa 1984. My friend Carolyn and I are posed on our brown, gold and white striped couch that has, thank goodness, long since been replaced. We are huddled together and my arm is draped around her shoulder. We are grinning like two goons.

She is lovely in her black, white and gold-trimmed holiday outfit; I am wearing my new red sweatshirt that says *Merry Me.* Her red hair is long; my dark locks are short and curly. We are both very thin.

Although the year is marked on the back of the photo, I would recognize it by my weight. I was determined not to enter forty fat. I didn't. Something happened on the way to fifty, however. But that's off my point.

The best part of this photograph is that we are, for no known reason other than the spontaneity of the moment, each wearing on our heads little stuffed Rodney Reindeers. Their long noses are pressed against our foreheads; their front legs drape over our temples and their hind legs hug the backs of our heads. We are as happy as can be. Buddies. We both love the Christmas season, in spite of its hassles.

We invited Carolyn and Farhad over for our annual Christmas gift exchange. I don't remember what we purchased for each other, but what we mainly gave each other, and continue to give, is joy. Always. I do not have another friend who likes to *play* (in the juvenile sense of the word, no holds barred) as much as I do, aside from Carolyn. Farhad also knows how to let it rip, and the four of us own some swell memories. Snowball fights. Sitting around our dining room table wearing wax mouths. Dinners out, laughing about how one of our teeth fell out—and I'm not telling whose, although he has a name uncommon here in the States . . .

125

Carolyn and I can be wonderfully silly together, and deeply profound. She is a family counselor, and I have called upon her expertise and listening ear on more than one occasion as I've worked through some difficult times in life. We met them the day they moved in next door in 1978.

We recently had a short visit with them on our back porch, before they returned to their new home in Colorado. We hugged, we laughed, we shared a quick beverage; time was too limited. I received the most wonderfully tender birthday card weeks later. It is as sacred to me as the Rodney Reindeer photo.

Lord, thank you for friendships that continue no matter what the distance.

*   *   *

How many times can the same cheese ball be served? That is the question of the moment. My (Hazel Smith's) Pineapple Cheese Ball is very tasty. (Mix 16 oz. cream cheese, 8 oz. drained crushed pineapple, 1 tsp. chopped onion, 1 tsp. seasoned salt. Roll ball in 2 c. chopped pecans.)

This cheese ball is also soft enough to re-roll (adding pecans in the bare spots) after portions of it have been attacked.

(Please tell me I'm not the only one who does this.) In fact, it can be patched and re-rolled several times. Once I got that puppy down to about two inches in diameter, but it still tasted great and looked perky enough for guests. It's all in the presentation; I have a darling Christmas platter.

It is with the shrinking cheese ball (which I did NOT learn about in the live demonstration) and the leftover portions of whiskied weenies and dips that some of my favorite Christmas moments are shared with friends. Spontaneous. Calls you make because the people popped into your mind, and, well, you have this cheese ball and all your decorations and . . . They are relaxed encounters. Intimate. Low-stress. Cups of tea steep; spiced wine warms; candles flicker (no dusting); stories are shared, memories perused. Dips are now spread on your mixed cracker assortment, which holds the last of each of the boxes. There is a quiet glow about these visits that endears them to me.

Thank you, Lord, for the miracle of the crackers and cheese ball that fed the multitudes.

* * *

There are times in our lives when, due to work deadlines and other pressures, inviting anyone to your home is just more than you can manage.

Maybe hospitality isn't your gift, and you dread entertaining more than you dread the thought of plucking nose hairs.

Maybe the people whom you feel obliged to invite have worn you down with bickering and petty gossip. Being around them opens wounds you'd rather not pick at.

Yes, there are times when holiday entertaining *needs* to be back-burnered; I am not suggesting we all need to turn into Martha Stewarts. And martyring ourselves rather than serving with happy hearts is not a Christian approach, nor does it honor God or do anything for your spirit.

I have lots of great memories of Christmas moments shared with friends at a nearby hot-dog place or Mexican restaurant. No one (aside from the restaurant workers) has to wash dishes, and sometimes we benefit from a change of scenery. We need to be around people who cheer us up, not tear us down, and if we must go out to find them, so be it.

Nor should you feel guilty when you simply cannot open your doors—or your heart—to guests, whether they're in or out of your home. Maybe it's all you can muster this holiday season to hang on to yourself.

But remember this: Inviting Jesus into your heart to share a quiet Christmas reflection takes no cooking or shopping or dusting or money. Asking the Lord to curl up with you in your favorite chair while you read about his birth in the Gospel of Luke, chapter two, calms the soul and reminds us what Christmas is really about.

For it is not until we are refreshed and replenished in the Lord that his lovingkindness can pass through us, bubbling out of us and into the lives of others during the Christmas season—or any other time of the year.

DAZE TWELVE

The Aftermath
(Tree-Needle Blues)

'Twas the day after Christmas
and all through the house
not a human was stirring
'cuz they were pooped
and basking in the afterglow

of
Christmas perfection.
Right.

*　　*　　*

Ah, the day after Christmas. Mary Beth is busy getting her family involved in quickly disassembling and packing away that dust-laden tree and all the Christmas paraphernalia. "Okay, it's over. I want it gone," she tells husband Dave.

Others, like my godmother, Johanna, and myself, hate to take down the decorations right away because it all seems so glitterless, so dull and empty then. We're just not ready to let go. So we wait until after New Year's and coax another week of sparkle out of our efforts. One year George and I were so late getting the tree down that I almost decided to add a bunch of hearts and call it the Valentine's Tree.

At dinner the day after Christmas, families enjoy the initial reheating of the succulent leftovers . . . before the realities of turkey sandwiches, turkey soup, turkey casseroles and turkey à-la-sick-of-it choke their way down throats.

Many, although they are very weary, are up at the crack of

dawn putting on their gym shoes and fanny packs, sharpening their elbows, gearing up to beat the throngs of frenzied people to the post-Christmas sales. Some dread the patience it takes to endure the hassles of exchanges and refunds. Then again, some are excited about exchanges and refunds because now they can actually get what they wanted. (Sometimes a cash refund will do nicely, thank you very much.)

A few household members will stay home, still entrenched in assembling new toys and appliances, looking for the remaining couple of pieces they're afraid got thrown away with the mess of Christmas wrappings. Others are trying to make room for the new stuff and beginning to worry that they might have to once again store it in the car trunk, where they hid it before Christmas, because there isn't a square inch of room anywhere in the house or apartment for yet more stuff, no matter how terrific and trendy it is.

When Brian was little, we needed to shift gears in order to prepare for his birthday, which is December 30. Our old friends' son, also a Brian, was born on Christmas Day. They used to change the tablecloth in late afternoon from Christmas to birthday. By the time overtired, overtaxed little Brian was seated at his birthday table, he hated everybody!

Post-Christmas Daze activities have a hustle and bustle of their own, and for a while we are swept along in their rhythm. But somewhere along the highway of commotion, it hits us that Christmas is actually over. We either did or didn't get what we wanted; family and friends either did or didn't come together; either joy or anxiety plagued us; Christ was or was not in our thoughts, activities, prayers; opportunities to make anything different—at least for this year—have passed us by. Thus, too, often begins the litany of If Onlys.

*   *   *

If only . . .

. . . the day after Christmas could be for lounging around instead of power shopping.

. . . we could have known the month before Christmas what we know the day after: that in spite of everything, Christmas will happen anyway, ready or not, and we will all, for better or for worse, survive.

. . . Uncle Jack didn't think it was so cute to give kids gifts that make noise.

. . . Uncle Jack's gifts would self-destruct.

. . . it was more than 365 days until this happens again.

. . . I hadn't eaten so much.

. . . school was back in session—*now!*

. . . we didn't have to disassemble all this Christmas stuff and pack it away.

. . . living-room floors had a Christmas Flush Knob. (Whammo! One big swirl and it's gone!)

. . . everything that needed batteries came with batteries.

. . . my family didn't have to fly home so soon.

. . . my relatives didn't know where I live.

. . . I wasn't alone.

. . . I didn't have so many people complicating my holidays—and my life.

*   *   *

If only I would remember to count my blessings rather than dwelling on what's wrong.

*   *   *

Sometimes I don't feel as if Christmas is *here* until after it's over, because that's when I finally have time to sit and stare into the depths of my Christmas tree or simply watch the streams of smoke rise and twirl out of the chimney of our miniature log cabin that burns pine incense. (Actually, we have two log cabins, a ceramic house and an outhouse with a smoke stack. Cute, huh? We could choke to death from essence-de-Christmas if I fired them all up at once!)

It's not that I don't look at the tree or light the incense before Post-Christmas Day; it's that I often don't have time to *really* notice their magic. Although just staring into a real tree after Christmas can knock needles to the floor, I often get the feeling that the ornaments come to life and gather together while we are sleeping (especially my singing hippopotamus, Christmas mice and dancing pig), share their stories, and hope that we will take time to listen to the sum total of their presence and meaning in our lives before we once again pack them away.

And oh, that pine incense! Fragrance has always been a potent and magical memory inducer. Like white clouds in the blue of sky and the little puffs of smoke that billowed from my brother's Lionel many years ago, the pine-laden spirals streaming from the log cabin capture my imagination as I watch them change course, round and flatten, stretch and twist in response to the invisible currents and forces that be.

"The smoke of the incense, together with the prayers of the saints, went up before God from the angel's hand" (Revelation 8:4). This verse comes to life with new visual meaning as I sit in stillness, inhaling this wondrous fragrance that I cannot see but for its trail of vapor.

So, too, Christmases—and all the days of our lives—disappear into time, leaving nothing behind but their memories. (And photo-developing bills.)

One year we experienced just about everything in our home:

* the last-minute "How will everything get done?" panic

* the magic of plugging the tree in for the first time and having all the strings actually light

* the sound of crashing ornaments as Wonderdog Butch (wearing a lampshade-shaped collar to keep him from licking his sore leg off) hooked two tree branches while hurtling through the house to bark at the UPS man

* bountiful food
* electronic gifts that didn't work
* gifts that were so perfect you wanted to cry (and so I did)
* family members home for the holidays
* the stomach flu

and surprises I would have never dreamed of, like that power drill Santa gave me.

It is only in reflection that they lock in on the corners of our hearts and bring a tear, a pang of guilt for a missed opportunity, or a smile.

*   *   *

Bret and his girlfriend are to arrive at O'Hare airport from Albuquerque at 5 p.m. Christmas Eve. Due to heavy fog, everything is delayed. The decision is finally made that George and Brian will head for the airport and I'll go to the 7:00 service to save seats. I haven't attended the children's presentation of the Christmas story for years, and I am thirsting to once again see it with the beauty and innocence of childlike eyes.

I sit in a row by myself and line up hymnals and bulletins on the pew to assure room for my family when they arrive.

Services begin. We sing; we hear a message. Finally cherubic children draped in gold garland begin to proceed down the aisle toward the front of the church. I am tingly with joy for the reenactment of the holy night and these beatific angels.

Imagine my surprise when the narrator introduces them as aliens from planet Zyron! *What? Aliens? Is nothing sacred?* I scream inside my head. *Why can't anything stay the same? Who would mess with the Christmas story?* I ramble to myself and fidget in my seat, but as it turns out, the out-of-this-world beings win me over. They present a perfect opportunity for other characters in the play to explain the Christmas story to the extraterrestrial visitors who know nothing about our Savior's birth.

Although I do enjoy the untraditional pageant and welcome the candlelight service to follow, I finally relinquish any hope of sharing this part of Christmas with my family. In fact, I am kind of bemoaning the fact that I'm spending Christmas Eve without them. Maybe I should have gone to the airport; at least we would be waiting together.

The congregation is asked to form a circle around the outer

perimeter of the sanctuary. We jostle our way into position, each holding an unlighted candle. The church lights dim and people on either side of the mass of candles burning in the front of the church tip their individual candles toward this great glow, readying to pass the flame, the light of Christ.

The flickering radiance reflects and dances on each face as the flame passes in front of their heart and lights the candle of the person next to them. Carefully and purposefully, the light spreads around the circle, from one of God's children to the next in this endless circle of Christmas love.

Just before the flame comes to me, the back door to the church opens—next to where I am standing—and in walks my family. We all nestle together in the corner in a mass of hugs and tears as we pass the light of Christ to complete the circle. Then the singing of carols begins.

It was a magic moment, and they are often best recalled in the quiet lull after the rush. Only then does it occur to you—to me—that God's timing is always perfect.

*　　*　　*

Whether it's the year of enchanted moments, like the one I

just described, or the first time a family member is missing for the holidays, one thing is certain: No matter what, "Jesus Christ is the same yesterday and today and forever" (Hebrews 13:8).

What we gather for our memory portfolios during the holidays and ponder in the aftermath is what either fills us with dread for next Christmas or feeds The Dream.

Throughout the holidays, the Holy Spirit beckons us to focus on the fact that in the beginning, Christmas was not announced by sale flyers and gabillions of cookies and electronic racing lights and to-do lists and forced greetings.

No. Upon the birth of his Son, God gifted us with the silent brilliance of a magnificent star and the words of an angel of the Lord. With the glory of the Lord shining all around, the angel told the shepherds, "Do not be afraid. I bring you good news of great joy that will be for all the people" (Luke 2:10). If you dwell on this throughout the holidays, then your post-Christmas memories will be rooted in holiness.

And those around you will have benefited as well, for you will be bursting with good tidings, and (as in the Gospel of old)

your message of Christmas—*in the midst of the chaos*—will be
 Glory to God in the highest heaven,
 and on earth peace among those whom he favors!
 (Luke 2:14 NRSV)

DATE DUE

GAYLORD			PRINTED IN U.S.A.

Charlene Ann Baumbich is enjoying her midlife years, spent mostly in working, taking estrogen and doing lunch. She is "*way* excited to be named the 1996 Celebrity Judge for White Castle's 75th anniversary recipe competition!" Charlene is a four-time author, conference and retreat speaker, and award-winning journalist who entertains and rejuvenates her listening and reading audiences with humor, uncommon wisdom and passionate insights. "I occasionally have brilliant thoughts," she says, "and love passing them on—whether they concern the good, the bad or the dubious."

To contact Charlene regarding a speaking engagement for your civic, church or professional group (or just to say hi), write or call

Charlene Ann Baumbich
22W 371 Second Street
Glen Ellyn, IL 60137
Phone: (630) 858-1091
Fax: (630) 858-1094
E-mail: Charstar1@aol.com